D1201180

PRAISE FOR *CRUSHING QUOTA*

I've read hundreds of books on coaching and leadership through the years, and I must say *Crushing Quota* is in a league of its own. It is the most practically useful book on sales coaching I've read. This is a must-read for those who are serious about sales coaching.

> —**Chris Dials,** Vice President, Global Operations, VMware

While there is no silver bullet to improving sales performance, coaching comes pretty close, and this is the best sales coaching book I've ever read.

> —**Doug Bushée,** Vice President, Sales Enablement, Xerox

Sales Playbooks and processes are foundational, but execution depends on a sales manager's ability to prioritize, apply them, and coach to clear outcomes. This book is all about that and is relevant for all sales processes and all sales roles. The research rigor and the practical framework is spot on and was something I could implement immediately. Ultimately, this book will help make any sales manager a top performer, and provides organizations looking to deliver sustainable and profitable growth the formula to succeed.

> —**Lotta Bager,** Director of Sales Excellence, QBE Insurance

Crushing Quota is an essential manual for sales organization improvement. It makes the case for salesperson coaching as sales management's most vital and overlooked contribution to firm performance, then offers a teardown of coaching's essential elements and a practical guide to implementing them. *Crushing Quota* stands alone as the definitive sales coaching guide.

> —**Bob Kelly,** Chairman, Sales Management Association

As a learning leader, I appreciate the applicability of this framework to the entire sales force. I have had the privilege of working with Michelle, Jason, and the Vantage Point team to successfully implement the practices outlined in *Crushing Quota* with measurable outcomes. The sales managers found the concepts relatable, providing fresh clarity to the sales process and renewed energy to coaching the sellers.

> **—Karen Basile,** Vice President of Enterprise Learning, Johnson Controls

Finally, a highly relevant and practical guide to sales coaching. A refreshing look at how research challenges conventional wisdom on this important topic.

> **—John E. Davis,** SVP Global Sales and Marketing, CryoLife, Inc.

Surely the quest of all sales leaders is outperformance in every area. In a world of rapid change and commoditization any competitive advantage should be leveraged to its fullest. My 28 years of professional sales leadership roles across four continents and leading teams of thousands in extremely complex and challenging environments has taught me that I can still improve.

So little credible research has been done in the world of sales leadership. Michelle and Jason have taken the lead in a critical area that needs constant analysis and review. This book is a must read for all soon to be and established sales leaders. The recommendations in this book provide a guide, that when applied, can facilitate a genuine positive change.

Conventional old school wisdom has lost the race against progress. Choose to make a positive difference while taking your team to outstanding sales performance. I highly recommend this book as a must-read.

> **— Paul Helmore,** Director of Global Accounts, Schlumberger

CRUSHING QUOTA

CRUSHING

Proven Sales Coaching Tactics for
Breakthrough Performance

QUOTA

Michelle Vazzana, PhD

with Jason Jordan

NEW YORK   CHICAGO   SAN FRANCISCO   ATHENS
LONDON   MADRID   MEXICO CITY   MILAN
NEW DELHI   SINGAPORE   SYDNEY   TORONTO

1 2 3 4 5 6 7 8 9   LCR   23 22 21 20 19 18

ISBN 978-1-260-12115-5
MHID   1-260-12115-1

e-ISBN 978-1-260-12116-2
e-MHID   1-260-12116-X

McGraw-Hill Education products are available at special quantity discounts to use as premiums and sales promotions or for use in corporate training programs. To contact a representative, please visit the Contact Us pages at www.mhprofessional.com.

I dedicate this book to my children, Nick and Anna.
They have given my life meaning in ways that business success
cannot touch. I thank God for them every day.

CONTENTS

FOREWORD

WHAT AN ODD THING IT IS

I 've always found sales coaching to be an oddity. It's something that everybody wants to happen and practically anyone can learn to do. Sales leaders expect their sales managers to coach. They invest in training to develop coaching skills. They even buy software to increase coaching effectiveness.

When you talk to sales managers, they tell you they like to coach, knowing the big difference it can make. And I can't tell you how many times salespeople have told me how much they want and need to be coached.

In short, everyone involved in sales supports coaching. It might be the only thing that's universally desired by every sales force too—other than crushing quota, of course.

Here's where the story gets odd. Sales coaching rarely happens. Repeated studies show that despite all the talk about its importance and value, sales managers rarely get around to it. Sales managers admit the fact, their leaders bemoan it, and their salespeople concede it. But sales trainers continue to train on coaching skills, and programmers continue to build coaching apps. Hoping . . .

What prevents this most desirable of activities from actually taking place? Why is sales coaching so unattainable, despite the world's universal affection for it? There are many reasons, but what follows are the three biggest ones that I've seen during my career as a salesperson, sales leader, sales trainer, sales speaker, and programmer. (OK, I've never actually been a computer programmer, but I've known quite a few.)

Lack of Accountability

One of the biggest deterrents to widespread sales coaching is the lack of accountability to which sales managers are being held. For the sake of discussion, let's think about accountability as having several different levels. First, you can ask people to do something, which is basically *not* holding them accountable. At the next level, you can *measure* whether or not they're doing what you requested. One step further, you can *compensate* them for doing the task. And finally, you can *fire* them if they don't do what you've asked, measured, and compensated them to do.

Now let's look at sales managers and coaching. It's alarming how infrequently sales coaching is measured—even in sales forces that claim that it's a top priority. Occasionally, I see companies that ask managers to log their coaching conversations in their CRM. And I've seen managers surveyed to determine whether coaching sessions are taking place. But I could tally the total number of times I've witnessed such efforts on the fingers of my left hand.

Only once in my career have I encountered a sales manager's compensation plan that included coaching as a performance metric. This shouldn't come as a surprise. If companies don't measure sales coaching, then they surely can't use it as a basis for incentive compensation.

As you can see, beyond asking managers to "do it," the level of accountability for sales coaching falls off pretty quickly. And who has ever seen a sales manager fired exclusively for not coaching his or her salespeople? No one. Ever.

In fact, it's almost laughable to think that an otherwise competent sales manager would be terminated for a lack of coaching effort. But who knows? Perhaps there's an unemployed, formerly accountable sales manager somewhere who can dispute my cavalier claim. But I doubt it.

Lack of Definition

The second reason I suspect that sales coaching doesn't take place is a general lack of understanding about what it really is. The definition of *coaching* is as nebulous as the definitions of a *sales process* or *sales enablement*. If I were sitting in front of you right now, how would you answer the question: What is *sales coaching*? Chances are, you'd define it as a management skill set or competency that leads to a specific outcome on the part of the seller—probably using words like "collaborative" or "developmental." Well, yes, but there's more to it.

For sales coaching to really take life in a sales force, managers and sellers need very specific parameters against which they can execute it. For example:

- When exactly should coaching take place, and where?

- What specific topics should be discussed, and why?

- What information should be brought to the conversation?

- What should be documented afterward?

- How should you measure the coaching process, as well as its impact?

In the absence of such details, sales managers are asked to coach with little more guidance than the simple missive to "just do it." It's therefore no surprise that sales coaching isn't a regular occurrence in most sales forces. Managers will happily *try* to just do it, but they quickly get lost without a clear set of instructions. As I said before, most sales managers do want to coach their reps, but their intentions fall victim to the ambiguity of the task.

Lack of Urgency

The final challenge I see to consistent and pervasive sales coaching is a shocking lack of urgency for it. Someone once said that coaching is the most important thing that doesn't have to happen by Friday afternoon. CRMs must be updated, for sure. Forecasts must be submitted. Expense reports must be signed. But coaching?

Here again, sales coaching is an oddity. *Everyone* tells you that it's important, and many argue that it's the most valuable role any sales manager can play. Yet it stands in line behind all the administrative and procedural roles that every sales manager *must* play: Are your forecasts always late? Fired. Expense reports out of compliance? Fired. Didn't coach your reps this week? No one even noticed.

If sales coaching is as important as we say it is, then it deserves a real sense of urgency. Perhaps coaching should be the first thing sales managers do each week, not the last thing they try to squeeze in before the weekend. Perhaps coaching should have a nonnegotiable deadline that must be met. Perhaps coaching salespeople should even be more urgent than submitting this week's forecast. Just maybe.

WHY I LOVE THIS BOOK

When Michelle asked me if I'd write this foreword, I thought, "Does the world really need another book on sales coaching?" After reading the pages that follow, I can confidently answer, "Yes!"

Crushing Quota is the antidote to the persistent coaching maladies described above. It gets to the nuts and bolts of powerful sales coaching. It defines what you need to do to be a great sales coach, as well as the when, why, and how of doing it. These insights are supported by years of solid research from Vantage Point on the dos and don'ts of effective sales management.

Better yet, *Crushing Quota* lays out a rock-solid business case for sales coaching that will ignite the fire of urgency. It also makes the coaching task finite enough for legitimate measurement and accountability. You won't need to pick through this book for the few credible moments of truth—you can take these lessons straight to the bank. Which is kind of the point.

Sales coaching is your ticket to success. It's the only way you can continually up-skill your entire sales force, which is an absolute necessity in today's ever-evolving business environment. In summary, *Crushing Quota* belongs on every sales manager's bookshelf as the definitive guide to sales coaching. If you want to become a better coach or develop real coaching capability in your sales force, then you must read on.

Sales coaching shouldn't be an oddity any longer. As something that's universally desired, it should be universally present in your sales organization. If you look around your sales force in a few years and see nothing but world-class coaches, *Crushing Quota* will be to blame.

—Jill Konrath
author of *More Sales, Less Time*
and *SNAP Selling*

ACKNOWLEDGMENTS

I'd like to acknowledge the tireless efforts of Phil Knowles, our founding partner, for his role in editing and reality testing both the content of this book and the research findings that fueled it. No matter how busy he was, he made time to review draft after draft of each chapter. He provided the voice of the sales manager to ensure that we kept the guidance tactical and practical.

I'd also like to thank Dr. Vincent Fortunato for his excellent and thoughtful guidance throughout the most critical stages of my dissertation and associated research project. He truly made the difference in my journey, and I owe the completion of my PhD largely to him.

I'd like to thank the many clients that participated in Vantage Point's research project. Without them, this book would not have been possible.

—**Michelle Vazzana**

I'd like to acknowledge our amazing colleagues at Vantage Point. Though we learn a lot from our major research projects, we learn even more from our daily interactions with bright, insightful coworkers who continually test our thinking and push our boundaries. Many of the ideas in this book could never be credited properly because they resulted from thousands of conversations with dozens of colleagues over years of collaboration. Thank you for anonymously powering our intellectual progress.

—**Jason Jordan**

CRUSHING QUOTA

PART I

COACHING: WHAT IT IS, WHAT IT ISN'T, AND WHAT IT COULD BE

CHAPTER 1

THE CASE FOR BETTER
SALES COACHING

If you are reading this book, you are either a sales manager who wants to become a better coach, or you are responsible for helping the sales managers in your organization become better coaches. Either way, this topic is important to you. Important enough to invest your time and energy in getting better at this critical sales management activity.

Our goal in writing this book is to give you practical, research-based guidance that will improve your ability to coach the right things, in the right way, at the right time. Our promise to you is that this will be the most practical and useful book on coaching you have ever read.

The first thing we want to make clear is that coaching matters. It is a game changer. This chapter makes an unassailable case for becoming a better sales coach.

THE SIZE OF THE COACHING PROBLEM

How big a problem is the current state of sales coaching? We all agree that managers are important. We've all seen good managers and bad—everyone wants to report to the good ones, and everyone wants to run from the bad ones. But unlike salespeople, sales manager performance often eludes quantification. What's the real value of good or bad managers? How do we know if they are doing their job well? One alarming trend getting our attention is that the percentage of salespeople at quota has been in a steady decline for the past six years. This is occurring at the same time revenue targets are on the rise.

> One alarming trend getting our attention is that the percentage of salespeople at quota has been in a steady decline for the past six years. This is occurring at the same time revenue targets are on the rise.

So how much does sales management matter? What kind of impact are sales managers having on their organization's ability to hit their revenue targets? What is the impact on revenue attainment when sales managers are not good coaches? After our last book *Cracking the Sales Management Code*, we turned our research toward these important questions and we discovered some interesting things. First, there's the most obvious measure of "good" managers, which is how they perform against their revenue targets. Here's what we found.

Figure 1.1 illuminates the significant impact sales management has on a firm's ability to achieve revenue targets. In the initial wave of our study that included over 600 sales managers, we identified a $3.5 million gap between the top 25 percent of managers and the lowest 25 percent. This is not a magic number. You can do the math for your own organization. In fact, one of our clients did their own math and came to a staggering $10 million gap between their top 25 percent of managers versus their bottom 25 percent. The statistic in Figure 1.1 assumes an average team size of 9.1 and an average quota of $1 million. It is quite easy to do this computation for your own organization. All you need is the average quota, average team size, and revenue difference between your top and bottom 25 percent of managers.

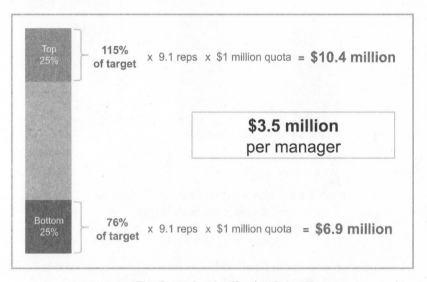

FIGURE 1.1 **The Cost of an Ineffective Sales Manager**
Source: Vantage Point Sales Management Practices Study. Note: n = 518.

This is not a theoretical projection. This is based on real numbers. We did the math, and the math scared us. We knew that sales managers were important. We knew that coaching mattered. Now we knew just *how much* coaching mattered. We were now in possession of facts that got our attention and the attention of sales leaders around the globe.

When we examined the managers in our Vantage Point Sales Management Practices Study based on revenue performance, the outcome was concerning. As expected, the top 25 percent of sales managers exceeded their revenue targets. The bottom 25 percent of managers fell short. No surprise there. As illustrated in Figure 1.2, the top 25 percent of sales managers were generating 39 percent more revenue than the bottom 25 percent. The core group of managers, the middle 50 percent, were hovering around quota. You might be thinking this is not such bad news, that the story isn't as scary as we have led you to believe. It is. Read on.

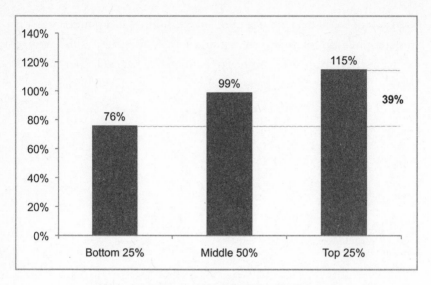

FIGURE 1.2 Sales Manager Revenue Performance in Relation to Revenue Target

Source: Vantage Point Sales Management Practices Study. Note: n = 518.

A question you might be asking yourself at this point is, "Is there another, more important measure of sales manager effectiveness? If so, what is it?" When we dug a bit deeper, we hit pay dirt. Although revenue attainment is vital, it is only one target by which a sales manager's effectiveness can be judged. Many organizations we encounter are now incorporating a new metric, one that gives better insight to overall manager effectiveness: the percentage of sellers on any given team who are making quota.

When we looked at the percentage of sellers on a given team making quota, across the different performance levels, we found something a bit shocking. As can be seen in Figure 1.3, there is a glaring gap between average and high performers. Although the top-performing managers produced 16 percent more revenue than the middle 50 percent, they got *over 30 percent more of their sellers to quota*. When we examined the data in this way, we saw the disparity between the top and middle performers in a whole new light. In fact, the middle 50 percent of sales managers were getting only slightly more of their sellers to quota than the bottom 25 percent of sales managers. How was it possible that that the middle-performing managers were getting 23 percent closer to their revenue target compared

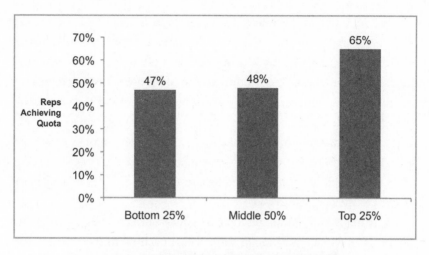

FIGURE 1.3 Sales Manager Performance Level
Source: Vantage Point Sales Management Practices Study. Note: n = 518.

with the lowest-performing managers, when *no more of their sellers were making quota?*

Well, logic would indicate that these middle-performing managers were either hitting their revenue targets on the backs of too few sellers, or they were playing the role of player-coach and were closing the gaps with their own selling efforts. If they were relying on a few high-performing sellers to hit their targets, what were they doing to improve the performance of the rest of the salespeople on their team? If they were doing the selling themselves, then it was impossible for them to devote adequate coaching time to close the performance gaps across the team. Either way, this was a bad-news scenario.

The cold hard facts demonstrate that sales managers are failing. These same high-achieving individuals who were successful salespeople are largely unable to replicate their high performance when managing a sales team. This is a travesty, both for the sales managers who are failing and for the organizations that employ them. Consider why this is particularly alarming. Sales managers are promoted because they are successful salespeople. When sales managers are failing, not only is the organization they work for at risk of not making their number but that same organization has also lost high-performing salespeople. It is a double hit.

On the one hand, it makes perfect sense to promote your best and brightest. It makes intuitive sense that your best salespeople would be the best candidate pool for your sales management population. However, this success as an individual contributor all too often doesn't translate to success in the sales manager role. In our study, 75 percent of the sales managers missed their revenue targets and were getting fewer than half their sellers to quota. Something is amiss. Why are so many managers failing? What can we do to address this problem, and where does sales coaching come into play? Are companies failing to equip their sales managers to coach? Do they not care?

As it turns out, companies do care about sales coaching. Leaders in most organizations care enough about sales coaching to train their managers how to do it.

HOW TRAINING COMES INTO PLAY

Figure 1.4 shows the top three topics that were identified in three separate needs analyses we encountered in our work with clients. In all cases, sales coaching emerged as either the first or second most important training topic for sales managers. This is not unique to the three organizations represented in this illustration. We conducted a joint study with the Sales Management Association to better understand how organizations trained their sales managers. Our study included 213 companies representing over 25,000 sales managers. As part of the study, we wanted to better understand which topics were deemed most important for sales manager training. We were not surprised to find that sales coaching rated number one in terms of importance. Companies in our study that conducted effective sales coaching training realized 8 percent more revenue compared to companies that didn't.

Our sales manager training study also revealed that organizations that heavily invest in training their sales managers perform better. But by how much? We were able to tease out just how big an impact investing in sales managers has on revenue performance. In addition to exploring the topics that organizations were training in, we analyzed the percentage of

1. **Coaching**	1. Business planning	1. **Coaching**
2. Setting standards and goals	2. **Coaching**	2. Strategic planning
3. Recruiting and selection	3. Setting the right measures	3. Performance management

FIGURE 1.4 Needs Analyses by Three Separate Organizations

sales training budgets that organizations allocated to sales managers versus salespeople. As you can see in Figure 1.5, companies that allocated more than half of their sales training budget to sales managers generated 15 percent more revenue compared to companies that invested less than 25 percent of their budget on this important audience.

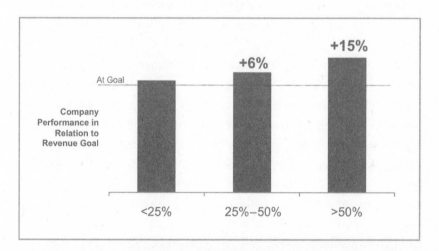

FIGURE 1.5 Percentage of Sales Training Budget Allocated to Management
Source: 2016 Joint Vantage Point and Sales Management Association Study. *Note: n* = 161.

At this point you may have reached the very sound conclusion that sales managers are important, sales coaching matters, and training sales managers to be better coaches is the obvious solution. It is always satisfying to reach sound conclusions, especially when those conclusions are supported by data; however, the best solutions are often not as obvious as they seem.

Herculean Training Effort, Minimal Results

One of our Fortune 50 clients had reached a similar conclusion, that training sales managers how to coach was important. This company's leaders were so committed to coaching that they put their sales managers through five different coaching training courses over a four-year period. When we calculated the hours of training across the sales management population, it amounted to 5,000 hours out of the field. Truly, this was a significant commitment to sales coaching. This organization wanted sales managers to coach, and they invested accordingly.

This level of investment in sales coaching training was sizable, both in terms of hard costs and time out of the field. It is reasonable to assume that managers who have been so well trained would certainly be effective coaches. It is also reasonable to expect that these very well trained managers would be *coaching* their salespeople. Well, unfortunately that was not the case.

Figure 1.6 illustrates the results of a survey that was deployed in this same company. Managers and salespeople were surveyed to determine how much coaching was happening. As you can see, the sales managers had a very different perspective on time spent coaching compared with the salespeople they managed. Over 90 percent of the sales managers reported coaching each of their salespeople *three or more hours* per month. Over 50 percent of salespeople reported getting *less than three hours* of coaching per month. That's a disparity of 49 percent between the manager

Hours per Month	Sales Manager	Sales Rep	Gap
<3	7%	56%	49%
3–5	55%	32%	23%
>5	38%	12%	26%

FIGURE 1.6 **Perception of Time Spent Coaching**
Source: Vantage Point client.

and seller perception of time spent coaching. These types of perception gaps are common, but what does this mean, and why does this happen?

Why the Discrepancy?

Well, there are at least two issues at play in this scenario. First, assuming that equipping a manager to coach will result in more coaching is dangerous. It is a false premise to assume that just because people know how to do something, they will do it. Anyone reading this book who has ever attempted to get in shape or lose weight knows this all too well. I may know how to exercise, and I may know how to eat right, but that doesn't mean I'm necessarily going to do those things. If my lifestyle is hostile to regular exercise or making healthy food selections, the going gets tough.

The same holds true for sales coaching. The managers in the above survey knew *how* to coach. They had been videotaped, audiotaped, and role-played to death as it related to sales coaching. The problem was that they couldn't coach because their environment was *hostile* to coaching. They couldn't figure out how to coach in any repeatable, predictable way in their current environment. Although managers cannot control the environment in which they operate, they can and do find ways to be more effective within that environment.

> The managers in the above survey knew *how* to coach. They had been videotaped, audiotaped, and role-played to death as it related to sales coaching. The problem was that they couldn't coach because their environment was *hostile* to coaching.

The second issue is that sales coaching is an ill-defined topic. The lack of a common coaching language creates all sorts of disconnects. When a sales manager is spending time talking with one of his salespeople, he generally assumes coaching is taking place. However, our survey data, as mentioned above, indicates that salespeople have a more critical ear relative to coaching. Without a common language, the coaching gap between managers and the salespeople they manage cannot close.

THE DRIVING FORCE FOR OUR RESEARCH

We are intimately familiar with this lack of sales coaching. We have worked with thousands of sales managers globally to help them become better sales coaches and operationalize coaching into the way they work. We have succeeded largely because we take an unconventional approach to coaching, one that challenges conventional wisdom. Our coaching research has revealed many surprising findings—findings that challenge well-entrenched beliefs that many of us hold dear about what constitutes effective sales management and coaching. We will unpack the details of our findings in subsequent chapters. Here, we want to help you understand the approach we used and what we were hoping to learn.

Although research has revealed that effective coaches outperform their less effective peers, no one has clarified what effective coaching is or how to do it. A study conducted in 2005 by the Sales Executive Council (SEC) revealed that managers who were rated as highly effective coaches outperformed managers who were rated as ineffective coaches by about 19 percent in revenue production. The problem with this type of information is that it isn't specific enough to be helpful. It makes us want to do better, but it doesn't tell us how.

We don't disagree with the SEC's finding that effective coaches outperform ineffective coaches. This principle holds true in all aspects of life, including sales. Our goal in conducting our own coaching research was to identify the actual coaching practices sales managers employ that result in a higher percentage of their salespeople achieving quota. Not generalities, but *actual practices*. We wanted to identify specific things managers could do to move the needle.

The Search for Answers

In order to get useful insights, we started with some overall questions to guide our inquiry. Below are some of the questions we sought to answer regarding high-performing sales managers and how they compared to their lower-performing peers:

- What types of interactions do they have with their reps? How frequently?

- What do they discuss?

- Do they generally have formal or informal interactions?

- Are certain discussion topics more closely related to success than others?

- Do they spend more or less time on forecasting and reporting?

- Are they spending more or less time in the field than lower-performing managers?

- When they coach, at what point in the sales cycle are they focused?

- When they spend time in the field, what types of sales calls do they attend?

- Do they spend more or less time in the field than your organization requires?

- Who initiates planning conversations (managers or reps), and what are the reasons?

- What level of planning rigor do they expect from their reps?

We spent over a year developing a survey instrument that reflected an appropriate level of detail to answer these important questions. We knew that we had 15 minutes or less to maintain management attention and collect details about their coaching practices. Figure 1.7 depicts the high-level methodology of our study that drove the design of our survey instrument.

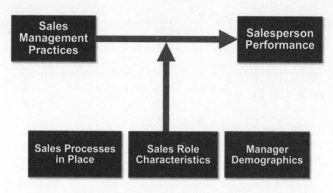

**FIGURE 1.7 Methodology for Comparing the Work Practices
of High- and Lower-Performing Sales Managers**
Source: Vantage Point.

We have collected data from over a thousand managers. We would like to report that we are finished, that the research is done, but that is not the case. As researchers, we answer some questions and others arise. So, alas, the research continues, the questions change, and the path to answers continues to evolve. The findings we share in this book regarding sales coaching are important, based on solid research, and specific. We are also candid enough to admit that there are always more questions, and we will remain curious enough to seek answers.

What You Can Expect

We would love to say that our research has unearthed the one right way to coach. That high-performing managers always exhibit the same best practices and those practices can be codified in a way that can remove all ambiguity and ensure success. But we did not find that *one way to coach*. In fact, the specific management practices differed greatly among organizations. We can't definitively say that the most successful sales managers coach each seller for five hours per month, spend one day per month with each seller in the field, and formally schedule their coaching interactions.

The reality is that there are many factors that affect coaching practices, and these factors render exact answers very difficult, if not impossible, to obtain. In some cases, we didn't find the answers we thought we would find. It would have felt good to find the secret sauce, the exact recipe. We didn't find it. We love to feel certain. Certainty feels good, but unfortunately it is often an illusion.

Although we did not find the one right way to coach, we found *patterns* high-performing managers exhibit. These patterns are real, they are consistent, and they hold true, time and time again. These patterns form the basis of the practical guidance you will receive throughout this book. It is likely that you will enthusiastically embrace some findings while you challenge others. Our hope for you is that you approach this book with an open mind and willing spirit. If you do, good things will happen. You and your sales team will benefit greatly. Let me share a quick story that warms our hearts and keeps us going when the going gets tough.

Going out with a Bang Instead of a Whimper

We often get pushback that tenured sales managers can't possibly benefit from coaching training. We understand the nature of the problem. It is a difficult sell to get 25-year veteran sales managers to attend training. If you can get them in a room, don't expect them to be enthusiastic about it. They've been there, done that, and that's all there is to it. We've encountered many of these grizzled veterans, and we're proud to say we've helped them. I'll share one case that stands out among the many.

While attending a national sales meeting with one of our key clients, we were approached by a sales manager named Mike. We'll omit his last name to protect his anonymity. Mike stopped us in the lobby of the hotel where the meeting was taking place, shook our hands vigorously, and thanked us for saving his ass. As you can imagine, we were immediately curious. We asked Mike to explain.

He proceeded to share the details of how he was on the bubble and dangerously close to getting on a performance plan. He was one of the veteran sales managers who participated in a coaching project we conducted with his company. He shared that he implemented the coaching practices he had learned, and those practices had made a meaningful difference for him and his team. He beamed as he told us that he had just returned from his company's president's club. He was proud of his accomplishment, and he attributed his turnaround to the types of practices included in this book.

This book is not about coaching 101. The practices we share in the following chapters apply to sales managers of all tenures and types.

A PREVIEW OF WHAT'S TO COME

- Chapter 2 explores the chaotic nature of the sales manager's job and why the transition from salesperson to sales manager is problematic. It creates the context for the discussion of the importance of establishing formal coaching practices.

- Chapter 3 examines the reasons that good coaching is not happening. We challenge prevailing wisdom regarding sales coaching and illustrate how organizations get it wrong when attempting to equip managers to coach.

- Chapter 4 introduces a research-based framework for selecting the best topics for coaching efforts. We explore our research findings regarding the type of coaching that leads to more salespeople at quota.

- Chapter 5 provides best practices for structuring and conducting coaching conversations. We introduce key elements of effective coaching discussions and provide a simple, yet powerful model for coaching conversations.

- Chapter 6 includes the common pitfalls managers encounter when attempting to operationalize coaching into their job. We offer specific guidance that managers can use to ensure that their coaching intentions are realized.

- Chapters 7 through 9 delve into the details of activity coaching, providing detailed content for conducting, structuring, and operationalizing territory, account, opportunity, and call coaching.

- Finally, Chapter 10 covers a few special cases to consider when developing your own coaching plan.

CHAPTER 2

WELCOME TO THE JUNGLE: THE SCARY REALITY OF SALES MANAGEMENT

As we highlighted in the previous chapter, sales management is a tough gig. Fewer and fewer sales managers are making a successful transition from high-performing salesperson to high-performing sales manager. One of the primary reasons managers fail to get more salespeople to quota is that their work environment is inhospitable to the behaviors needed to drive better sales performance. Coaching is critical. Coaching matters. And yet, so little good coaching is happening. Managers want to succeed. They want to coach, yet they can't figure out how. Why not? What's wrong?

This chapter illuminates the realities of sales management and how organizations unintentionally set managers up for failure. We highlight the practical realities sales managers face that impede their coaching efforts. We explore what this journey into sales management entails and why it is often wrought with potholes. We do this so that if you are a sales manager reading this book, you will know we understand your world. If you are a leader looking to help your sales managers, we offer insights that can help you reduce the distractions that impede manager effectiveness.

To illustrate the reasons for this struggle in a useful, practical way, I'm going to introduce you to Nick, a newly promoted sales manager, whose journey we will follow at various points throughout the book. We will share coaching practices that transformed Nick from an overwhelmed, ineffective sales manager to a true leader of his sales team. But the journey wasn't smooth. Nick got a rough start. The following narrative details Nick's first three months as a sales manager and sheds light on why this transition is hard.

THE ROCKY TRANSITION TO SALES MANAGER

Nick's a pretty typical sales manager. He's been in sales ever since he was hired by a high-tech manufacturing company right after he finished college eight years ago. Nick was well trained. And he's motivated—so much so that he made president's club six out of his eight years in sales, and he exceeded his quota the other two. Nick is much admired by his peers and managers alike. He always has a great attitude, and he is always willing to lend a hand to colleagues who need help.

During Nick's seventh year at the company, he was tapped for a future leadership role. His company is very intentional about leadership selection and preparation. Nick was enrolled in the management readiness program (MRP). He received additional leadership training and survived five rounds of panel interviews over a 12-month period before being deemed leadership ready.

Nick's Training

As part of his management preparation, Nick attended a supervisory training course. The first day was focused on self-assessment. It helped Nick understand his personal communication style, both under stress and in business-as-usual situations. He discovered that his communication became dominant and directive when he was under stress. He also discovered, not surprisingly, that this was not conducive to effective coaching. Not many of us shine under stress, after all.

He then learned that effective coaching is concrete and laser focused on discrete behaviors. He learned how to identify and mitigate performance gaps and how to use powerful interpersonal coaching conversations to help struggling employees get back on track.

He learned that his management approach with recent hires should be different from his approach with seasoned veterans, that they respond to different communication styles—which certainly made sense. He studied the powerful *Goal, Reality, Options, and Way Forward* (GROW) *model* for conducting coaching conversations. The idea of starting with the Goal, examining the current Reality, considering discussion Options, and then selecting a Way Forward made perfect, logical sense.

Nick was now armed and dangerous. He enjoyed the training immensely, particularly the part that enabled him to better understand his inherent strengths and limitations related to coaching. He felt well prepared to help solve performance problems that might arise. And he had a path to follow. All that remained was to put this great information into practice.

By the time Nick took the job as frontline sales manager, he was ready for the promotion. Or so he thought. Like so many sales managers, Nick had taken the job so he could help others achieve the type of success he had enjoyed. He intended to develop a whole team of superstars as a testament to his talent and his commitment to the company. He had always enjoyed coaching others. Now he could do it in earnest. Nick had great aspirations and plenty of commitment. He was going to make a difference as a sales manager.

Nick's Reality Hits Him in the Face

Nick's first 30 days in the new job were a blur. He spent a lot of time getting to know his team members, spending one-on-one time with each. He also spent time with his fellow managers, hoping to learn the ropes from the old hands. He became familiar with leadership's expectations, especially regarding the kinds of reports they wanted. The sheer volume of reporting was admittedly daunting, but he chalked it up to a learning curve that would certainly ease in time.

Another surprise was the amount of attention required by other departments outside of sales. Marketing, in particular, was always wanting information, much of which he had to get from his team. By the end of his first month, Nick was exhausted—but still excited. Surely this would get easier and more "doable" with time.

Fast-forward to the end of month 2. Nick had still not found a way to reduce the administrative burden. On a typical day, he was in the office by 7 a.m. and not out until 6 p.m. By arriving early, he could at least get a head start on the e-mails that continuously flooded his inbox. Everyone seemed to want his attention. Most days his team members arrived and started knocking at his door before he'd made a discernible dent in his e-mails.

Unfortunately, his attention was always divided. He could never really focus on any one thing. When he was with his salespeople, he was constantly thinking about all of the administrivia that wasn't getting done. When he was responding to e-mails or doing the required reporting, he always had the uneasy feeling that he wasn't attending to his sales team—which is what he had been hired to do!

By the end of month 3, Nick was beginning to get depressed. He was spending far too little time doing the coaching he anticipated when he took the job. His management training seemed a distant memory, and quite frankly it seemed entirely unrelated to what he was doing on daily basis. He was also spending less time in the field than he had hoped. He felt reduced to attending only sales calls where big deals were on the line and he was expected to help get them closed. In truth, he wasn't doing much coaching at all. But he still loved being in the field interacting with customers. After all, that's what led to his meteoric success in the first place.

As Nick sat in the office late one night, he reflected on all of the preparation he'd received in the MRP. He'd received diversity training, conflict resolution, interviewing skills, how to conduct performance appraisals, and how to deal with performance problems. Unfortunately, none of this great stuff had prepared him for what he'd experienced thus far. The vast gulf between what he'd expected and what he was experiencing was shocking. He wondered if perhaps he'd completely misunderstood what he was getting into. Was he naïve? Was leadership not all it was cracked up to be? Was he just not cut out for this role? These questions plagued him. He had no answers, only more and more questions.

Questions, questions, and more questions presented themselves. What if he wasn't up to the job? What if his salespeople didn't make quota? What if he could never coach them the way he wanted to? What was his boss thinking about his performance thus far? Was he not really the rock star that his prior performance indicated? Was someone going to figure out that he didn't really know what he was doing in this new job? Yikes, so many things to worry about. And what about the 200 unanswered e-mails from just the past week?

Nick honestly felt that no matter how hard he worked, no matter how many hours he put in, he could not get ahead of this situation. E-mails continued to pile up, demands from his boss continued to rise, his team needed his guidance and help, and customers were increasingly demanding. Nothing he'd learned in his 12-month sales management readiness program had prepared him for the reality of the job.

Before he knew it, three more months had passed. Where had the time gone? Why had his training not equipped him to handle the realities of the sales manager job? Time continued to fly, and Nick's confidence continued to wane. He continued to be plagued by questions, answers to which were not forthcoming. Maybe, just maybe, he should consider going back into sales as an individual contributor. Nick had never really failed at anything since joining the company. He certainly didn't want to give up, but he really couldn't figure out how to do everything necessary and still coach his team members.

Nick was failing, and he didn't know what to do about it.

THE CHAOS OF SALES MANAGEMENT

Why was a successful transition from salesperson to sales manager so elusive for Nick? Is this an unusual situation, or are many other first-time sales managers facing the same plight? Our experience suggests the latter, almost to a manager. The real demands of the job tend to squeeze out most of the room for actual coaching. In fact, the environment seems to be downright *hostile* to coaching.

But why? Why is the development of individual sellers so often and so easily abandoned given that managers have both a strong desire and powerful incentive to coach their sellers? Why do good intentions not get realized? The answer lies in the environment itself. Even very sophisticated organizations unwittingly create the very problems that prohibit effective coaching. Sales managers operate in a pressure cooker. Pressure is exerted from every direction, and it doesn't let up.

> Even very sophisticated organizations unwittingly create the very problems that prohibit effective coaching.

Let's examine these pressures on sales managers and the unfortunate consequences they spawn. Figure 2.1 illustrates the multitude of pressures exerted on sales managers. Understanding the pressures will not necessarily reduce them or lessen their impact, but it might lead to a better understanding of the real picture. If we can wrap our arms around the reality, we can perhaps set reasonable, realistic expectations regarding sales coaching. We can help managers thrive in a chaotic world—but not in the traditional way. Let's begin with the harsh realities of the sales manager's role.

FIGURE 2.1 The Sales Manager's Harsh Reality

The primary and most unrelenting pressure comes from *sales leaders*. Their insatiable appetite for data is strong, almost primal. The forecast is to a sales leader as lobster is to a foodie. It is a tasty treat. And limitless consumption is not merely acceptable but desirable. Accuracy is rewarded. Accuracy is demanded. But why this insatiable appetite? Why do sales leaders demand weekly forecasts, even while very little changes from week to week? Why is so much leadership time consumed by the creation and dissemination of the forecast? The career path of the typical sales leader might shed some light on this problem.

Consider the usual trajectory of a sales leader. She began as an individual contributor, a salesperson. As a salesperson, she had tremendous control over her actions and her results. She was largely in charge of her own destiny. Her success, much like that of our manager Nick, propelled her into a frontline sales manager role. Now she was no longer in control. Her success depended upon the performance of the 10 salespeople reporting to her.

Chances are good that many of the salespeople she managed were not quite as talented, or successful, as she'd been. One way to gain back some measure of lost control was to spend copious amounts of time in the field, helping to close deals. This ensured a higher likelihood of success. It was hard work helping 10 sellers achieve quota, but she was a superwoman after all. Ignore the fact that she was working 60 hours per week. What really mattered was that she had made president's club. Life was good. She was promoted again.

This time she was a manager of managers, a second-line sales leader. She no longer had the luxury of going on sales calls on a regular basis. She was further and further removed from the real action. While this series of promotions may look appealing on the surface, it is hell for a sales leader. Why? Because of control—or rather the lack thereof. The second-line sales leader is no longer in control of her own success. She is two layers removed from the field. She doesn't really know what's going on day to day, what the frontline sellers and sales managers are doing.

This lack of information is unsettling. Insecurity creeps in. Real control is now a distant memory. Well, by golly, if she can't be in the field, she can certainly be in the know by obtaining more and more information from her sales managers about what *they* are doing and what their *salespeople* are doing. The information she desperately craves is about the pipeline: which deals are closing and when. This information is comforting. In fact, it is so comforting that the desire to obtain it and examine it typically exceeds what is necessary and sufficient. The continual flow of information is not left to chance. It is scheduled, repeatable, and predictable. It's what allows sales leaders to sleep at night. Can you blame them? We can't. Everyone wants some semblance of control.

Human resources is another source of pressure that adds to the sales manager's burden. Human resources departments are commonly responsible for ensuring that the right salespeople get hired and trained. Often this is done by developing very sophisticated competency models for each role within the sales force. This allows the organization to achieve some level of predictability in the hiring, development, and assessment of salespeople.

Much of the burden of assessing and developing salespeople rests on the shoulders of the sales manager. While the logic behind competency models is strong and their place within organizations is well established, frontline sales managers do not embrace these models with the vigor that their human resources counterparts would prefer. Why? Well, assessing salespeople against a competency model seems very far removed from the everyday activities in which sellers engage. Sales managers often view competency models as disconnected from their day-to-day reality. Assessment is viewed as just *one more thing* a sales manager must fit onto an already overfull plate.

Marketing is another function that places demands on the sales manager. New products are being launched. New campaigns run. Demand must be created to increase sales and improve market share. To make sure the desired growth targets are met, marketers need information. They don't trust the information in the customer relationship management (CRM) system so they want it scrubbed. And they want it scrubbed by the sales managers. Requests for information for new product launches are not optional. Sales managers must comply. This is just one more demand on the sales manager's time.

Sales operations has another set of demands. Typically, the sales operations function is responsible for making sure the sales force has what they need to succeed. Tools and systems are purchased and deployed to ensure productivity on the front line. Tools and systems come at a very high price, and usage matters. Sales managers are constantly judged on

CRM and tool usage, and they are regularly reminded where they stand. The battle cry from sales operations is, *"Use the CRM, and clean the data."* After all: garbage in, garbage out. You know the story.

Customers need attention. They have billing issues, service issues, and other problems that need resolution. *Salespeople* want help dealing with customer issues. They want and need help strategizing deals, putting together proposals, determining pricing, navigating internal resources, and so on. The list goes on and on and on.

By this point in our discourse, the life of a sales manager may seem bleak—all these pressures and no real ability to reduce them or make them go away. This creates a feeling of helplessness within the sales manager. The inability to meaningfully improve the situation takes a toll.

The conundrum for sales managers is that the very reason they took the job, to help their salespeople succeed, is often last on the list of things that get attention. Sales managers desperately want to help their salespeople succeed, to help them achieve the same level of success they achieved, or more! The problem is that all the other demands placed on sales managers reduce their availability to do the main job for which they are held responsible.

Sales managers live in a reactive world. A sales manager could work 20 hours per day and still not complete all the necessary tasks. He could navigate the day and work like a maniac without making a single proactive decision. Just keeping up with the multiple and varied demands of others is an exhausting, yet unachievable goal.

Figure 2.2 reflects findings from a time study conducted by Dr. Adam Rapp, the executive director and professor of sales at Ohio State University. Dr. Rapp revealed that *at best*, managers spend about 32 percent of their time managing their sales team. The other 68 percent of the managers' time is consumed by managing information, administration, and direct customer interaction. If managers have only 32 percent of their time to manage their team, how on earth can they be expected to coach each seller for three to five hours per month? It seems like a utopian ideal, not a realistic expectation. And yet, there are managers who are laboring under just that expectation. How is this possible given the realities of the sales managers' role?

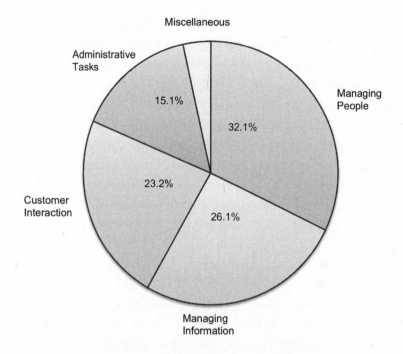

FIGURE 2.2 Sales Manager Time Study

Source: Adam Rapp with Doug Hughes, Andrew Peterson, and Jessica Ogilvie, "A Question of Productivity and Performance: The Selling Sales Manager or the Managing Sales Manager?" Thought Leadership on the Sales Profession Conference, Harvard University, June 5–6, 2012.

A LIGHT AT THE END OF THE TUNNEL

The reality of the sales managers' job is that it is hard. Really hard. The myriad pressures being exerted on sales managers, from all sides, create a chaotic environment that is difficult to navigate. Precious little time is available to manage and coach the sales team, and managing the sales team is the primary role of the sales manager. Some managers figure out how to survive and thrive in this environment, but most don't.

This plight of the sales manager, and our journey with Nick, may make you want to turn tail and run. Surely this sales management thing is a losing proposition. Not so fast. Fret not. Nick's story didn't end here, nor does this scenario need to continue to play out for most sales managers.

The picture got brighter for Nick. The obvious question is, how could many of the difficulties he encountered have been avoided? How can sales managers improve their journey and avoid the most common pitfalls along the way? How can sales managers go from almost no coaching to coaching consistently and doing so very effectively?

It is possible for sales managers to make this journey successfully. There are key insights that can help sales managers behave differently in their day-to-day job. If managers can get the right guidance, this transition from salesperson to sales manager can be smoother, take less time, and be less traumatic. This guidance is not rocket science. It is practical, actionable, and well researched. We provide this guidance throughout the rest of this book.

> If managers can get the right guidance, this transition from salesperson to sales manager can be smoother, take less time, and be less traumatic.

By applying the practices in the chapters that follow, amazing things can happen. Implement these tactics, and your salespeople will love you, your numbers will skyrocket, your spouse will love you again, and your hair will regrow. Well, maybe not the hair. But we know, unequivocally, that these practices work. We've done our homework. We have researched this coaching topic thoroughly. We've tested our methods. We know they work.

The proven coaching practices in this book will help you get more of your salespeople to quota. These practices will ensure that the coaching effort you expend will create significant value for the salespeople you manage. You will learn how to do better coaching, with less effort. We will help you avoid common pitfalls that dramatically impede coaching effectiveness.

We take you on a journey that can transform sales coaching from an amorphous idea to a predictable, repeatable element of your job. Our goal with this book is to shorten the journey from initial promotion to productive sales management. We unpack the hurdles and insights to help you chart a more direct path to effective sales management. We do this by focusing on the most important thing you can do as a sales manager: provide powerful, relevant coaching to your salespeople.

Whether you are a newly promoted sales manager or a grizzled veteran, this book will help you demystify sales coaching.

CHAPTER 3

SALES COACHING: HOW IT'S WRONG AND WHY IT FAILS

The title of this chapter may seem a bit gloomy. How sales coaching is wrong and why it fails seems a bit pessimistic. We agree. However, if you had had the opportunity to interact with as many sales managers as we have, if you had seen as many training initiatives fail, and if you had seen the widespread cynicism we've seen regarding sales coaching, you would most likely feel the same way. The good news is that many of the pitfalls we've seen can be avoided or at least repaired. We feel that giving you a better understanding of what doesn't work will help you more effectively act on what does work.

This chapter examines the most common barriers to effective sales coaching. We share real stories of efforts gone wrong so that you can learn from the mistakes of others and hopefully not waste precious time or resources. We start by addressing the most typical realities regarding sales coaching. We then move on to the path many organizations take to equip managers to coach and why they miss the mark. We explore some of the most typical barriers to coaching, including the sales manager's mindset. We end this chapter with a call to action regarding the best way to approach sales coaching.

THE CURRENT STATE OF AFFAIRS

Here's what coaching looks like for most sales managers. You attend a sales call with one of your sellers, you take detailed notes on what occurs, and you conduct a debrief in the car on the way back to the office. Coaching done. This has been and continues to be the conventional wisdom on how best to coach a salesperson. Get into the field as often as possible, spend as much time as possible with each of your reps, and consider yourself a champion coach. Unfortunately, this outdated view of coaching is no longer viable for two compelling reasons.

First, there is a practical reality that prevents most sales managers from spending more and more time in the field. One trend we've observed is that the ratio of salespeople to sales managers is growing. Another is that teams tend to be more geographically dispersed. When you combine a greater number of direct reports with a more dispersed geographic footprint, it's easy to see why field time is becoming more of a luxury than a go-to approach. Yet that's not the biggest challenge to our outdated view of coaching.

The biggest and most surprising reason that yesteryear's get-in-the-field-as-much-as-possible coaching strategy is a bust is that new research proves that it simply doesn't work! As I mentioned in the first chapter of this book, we expected to find certain things that we didn't find. One of the biggest surprises was that time and time again, lower-performing managers reported spending more time in the field compared to their high-performing counterparts. Not only were lower-performing managers spending more time in the field, they were spending more time in the field *than their organizations required.* Yikes.

The actual number of hours managers reported coaching their salespeople differed significantly from company to company; however, the pattern remained consistent. Whether it was coaching in the field or coaching in the office, the highest-performing managers were not coaching *more.*

Figure 3.1 shows the overall average hours per month spent coaching for the top 25 percent of managers in our study versus their lower-performing peers. You can see that there is a big disparity in coaching time, with the low performers reporting that they coach 27 percent more hours per month than the high-performing managers. This finding is surprising, and it goes directly against conventional wisdom that more coaching is better.

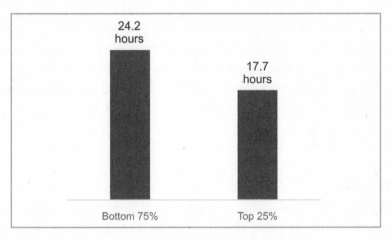

FIGURE 3.1 **Average Hours Spent Coaching**

We will introduce the specifics of what high-performing managers do differently in the following chapters. In this chapter, we will explore some of the primary reasons that much of the coaching that *is* being provided *isn't* being done effectively. We intend to help you avoid these common pitfalls.

HOW MANAGERS ARE
PREPARED TO COACH

To better understand why good coaching isn't happening, it is useful to step back and reflect on how organizations go about the important task of equipping their sales managers to coach. Significant efforts are expended on the important topic of coaching, and diving into the specifics of those efforts can give us a clearer picture of the coaching problem.

Sales managers are often trained to coach, particularly in large companies. In Chapter 1, we shared a story about one of our large clients who provided five separate coaching training courses. Despite being so well trained, these managers were doing very little coaching. Most salespeople want to be coached. Most sales managers want to provide coaching to their salespeople. So why are so many training programs and coaching models falling flat? We have wrestled with this thorny question for many years and have some insight as to the nature of the problem.

The way most sales managers are taught to coach does not represent the reality they face on the job. Managers walk away from training motivated to use what they've learned. They have the best of intentions. Then reality hits. It is not the sales managers' fault. There are valid reasons why well-intended training programs don't lead to good coaching practices. Read on.

General Leadership Models

When we work with clients to establish better coaching practices, we always examine the types of coaching training and coaching models they have deployed to their sales managers. We do this to better understand their sales managers' frame of reference for coaching. If a specific model has been deployed within an organization *and* it is being actively used, we do our best to incorporate that model into a broader framework. All too often, the models that have been deployed are not being used. I will explore two of the most common leadership models because we encounter them frequently in our work with clients.

GROW and Situational Leadership are excellent coaching models, frequently taught to managers (regardless of function), and they allow organizations to establish a common coaching framework. When we ask sales managers whether they *like* these models, they always say yes. When we ask them if they *use* these models, they say no. They liked the training they received, and they thought the models were interesting. They just didn't use them. Why? Let's start by better understanding each model and what it does.

GROW is an acronym that represents the *Goal* of the coaching discussion, the present *Reality* the employee is facing, the *Opportunity* for improvement, and a specific *Way Forward* to close the performance gap. It is a nice, clean, easy-to-remember way to orient a coaching conversation. The reason it doesn't get used is because the GROW model is better suited for addressing performance problems than it is for helping salespeople pursue and win deals.

Managers occasionally have performance conversations with their salespeople, particularly when they are conducting some type of formal review; however, this often represents fewer than 5 percent of the conversations managers have with their salespeople. The GROW model is ideal for conducting performance reviews. It is *not* as ideal when a salesperson needs help planning for an important sales call or developing a compelling proposal. Imagine a sales manager helping one of her sellers put together a proposal. What would that sound like using the GROW model? Let's try this out:

Manager: Well, what is your Goal for this proposal?

Seller: Ummm . . . I want to win the deal.

Manager: Of course. But what is the Reality?

Seller: I'm not sure what you mean. The Reality is that I have to put together this proposal, and it is due on Friday.

Manager: Yes, but how about the Opportunity. What is the Opportunity?

Seller: Well, it is a $50,000 deal, and it could help me hit my monthly quota.

Manager: That's true. So, what is your Way Forward?

Seller: I want to put together a proposal that increases my chances of winning this deal. I thought that was what we were going to discuss. Hey, did you just go to another of your manager training classes?

Obviously, we had a little fun with the above example, but it highlights why GROW is not applicable to many *real sales conversations* managers have with their salespeople. It is excellent for performance reviews, goal setting, and addressing performance problems. It is not as relevant for everyday sales coaching on how to win more deals. My intent is not to bash GROW but to highlight why it is often not applicable to sales coaching. Now, let's examine a second common leadership model we often encounter, Situational Leadership.

Paul Hersey and Ken Blanchard's Situational Leadership model is an excellent framework, and it has been in the marketplace for many years. It is a model that, like GROW, is typically deployed across an entire organization. Situational Leadership guides managers to adjust their approach to coaching and communication based on their employees' level of competence and commitment. Coaching behaviors are then adjusted accordingly to be more, or less, directive or supportive. It is a useful framework to orient *how* a manager is communicating with a salesperson; however, it doesn't address *what*, *why*, or *when* to communicate.

I often say that using Situational Leadership to coach is somewhat like using a weather forecast to determine what to wear. You can use the forecast to learn if it will be warm or cold, rainy or sunny, on a given day, but the forecast won't tell you what to wear—a tuxedo or a track suit. In order to determine what you will wear, you have to consider where you are going and what you are doing. Without that critical bit of information, you can't make an effective decision on what to wear.

Similarly, Situational Leadership will guide a manager on how best to communicate with a given employee—directing, coaching, supporting, delegating—as appropriate, but it will not tell the manager *what* to say, *why*, or *when* to have a coaching conversation. The problem is that this communication model is content free. It doesn't provide guidance on the concrete elements of a coaching conversation: what will be discussed, why, and when.

Although the GROW and Situational Leadership models are both widely taught, they are rarely used by the sales managers who learn them. They just don't resonate with the realities of sales management. Each model has its merits, and it is not surprising that organizational leaders include them in their management curricula. It is also not surprising that they are rarely used considering how *disconnected* they are with the types of coaching that form the bulk of conversations managers have with the salespeople they manage. If we look beyond general leadership models to sales-specific coaching models, we see similar issues with practical usage.

Sales-Specific Coaching Models

Organizations often provide sales managers with coaching training aligned to a sales methodology. If you are a sales manager reading this section, you are probably thinking back to the myriad coaching training sessions of this ilk that you have attended over the years. Your credenza most likely includes a few of the binders that house the tools included with those programs. You may look upon these binders fondly from time to time; however, that's pretty much were it ends. Here's why.

When an organization trains their salespeople on a given methodology, whether it be SPIN Selling, Strategic Selling, IMPACT Selling, Counselor Salesperson, the Challenger Sale, or any other sales methodology, there is always a companion coaching model. Sales managers receive training on how to coach to the sales methodology to ensure effective reinforcement after the salesperson training is complete. This sales coaching component typically involves a model for effective collaboration while coaching to the applicable methodology, a set of tools or guidelines for coaching to the methodology, and some expectation for frequency of coaching interactions. When viewed individually, these coaching programs appear highly effective, and they seem to provide a solid means of reinforcing the applicable sales methodology. Where they go awry is the way in which they are (or *are not* in most cases) operationalized into the managers' day-to-day reality.

For example, many organizations train their salespeople on *multiple* sales methodologies. A single organization may have trained their salespeople on SPIN Selling, Strategic Selling, and the Challenger Sale. Each of these sales methodologies includes a companion coaching model. Now instead of one coaching model and set of coaching tools, the managers have at least three to contend with and figure out how to incorporate into their day-to-day job. They are expected to coach to SPIN Selling, Strategic Selling, and now to the Challenger Sale. Well, which model is the right one? Do the managers coach to all of them? If so, how often? What are the criteria the managers can use to make this determination? It is easy to see why this is enormously confusing to sales managers and why it creates more confusion than clarity regarding sales coaching.

When Coaching Models Collide

If we assume that sales managers have been exposed to at least three sales methodologies as well as the two general leadership models, the sales managers now have *five* coaching models to reconcile. When do the sales managers use GROW? How about Situational Leadership? And what about when to coach to SPIN Selling, Strategic Selling, or the Challenger Sale? The managers will wrestle with this issue for only so long before giving up entirely and going back to the status quo. The more tenured the sales managers, the more problematic this becomes. It results in more binders on the sales managers' shelves, more coaching guides at their disposal, and in today's environment, more plug-ins within their CRM. Sales managers know that if they just keep their head low, they will outlast the flavor of the month and things will go back to normal after the dust settles.

Managers don't typically lack for coaching models and tools. What they lack is a way to effectively *integrate* these seemingly disparate pieces into a workable whole. One sales manager shared with us that his organization continued to provide him with individual coaching ingredients, when what he really needed was a workable coaching recipe. In addition to providing too many disparate coaching models, managers have many different types of coaching they are expected to conduct with their salespeople.

HOW SALES MANAGERS COACH
(OR DON'T COACH)

If we consider the broad range of coaching conversations sales managers can have with a salesperson, it provides more fodder for confusion. Let's explore some of the most common types of coaching that can and do occur. Below is a short list to consider:

- **Career coaching:** Coaching sellers to map out a career progression.

- **Behavioral coaching:** Coaching sellers to improve discrete sales behaviors such as questioning and objection handling.

- **Strategic coaching:** Coaching sellers to develop an appropriate approach to a territory, account, or opportunity.

- **Skills coaching:** Coaching sellers to improve specific sales skills such as questioning, prospecting, or cold-calling. Very similar to behavioral coaching. Most often associated with preparation and execution of sales calls.

- **Coaching to a competency model:** Similar to both behavioral and skills coaching but typically associated with the output of a competency assessment and associated development plan.

- **Performance coaching:** Coaching a seller to close a performance gap. This could be a revenue deficit, lack of compliance with activity targets, or some other deficit.

Which ones are *sales coaching*? How often should managers be conducting career coaching conversations? Do those conversations include some assessment against a set of competencies? Are specific behaviors associated with the competencies? Are the behaviors aligned to specific skills? Are the skills and behaviors aligned to the sales methodologies? Is a manager expected to use the GROW model or the Situational Leadership model when conducting these conversations? If so, when? Ugh!

When we look at the realities of how managers are equipped to coach, it is not surprising that very little coaching is happening. The example I shared in the first chapter about the huge gap between manager and seller perception of time spent coaching starts to make sense.

We recently encountered a global company that was struggling with this same issue. Coaching wasn't happening. Their solution? They deployed a very popular behavioral coaching model across the entire sales management population. This model was oriented toward sales behaviors and included very detailed tools to help managers conduct effective interpersonal coaching sessions with their sellers. This model was sales specific and comprehensive. We were impressed with the rigor with which this model was deployed.

The surprise came when we asked the sales operations manager how the organization gauged the success of the deployment. We expected to hear something along the lines of improved close rates, shorter sales cycles, increased sales of new products, or higher account retention. What we heard shocked us. We were told that the success of the deployment was measured by the percentage of salespeople who had a formally documented development plan. Huh? They don't have to sell more stuff? Nope. They just need to have a formally documented development plan? Yep. Wow, no small wonder adoption dies a quick death once reality sets in. When we asked how these development plans were specifically linked to business outcomes, the conversations died quickly.

So, we have issues with a common framework for sales coaching, confusion regarding the different types of coaching beyond just sales coaching, and a lack of linkage between coaching models and business outcomes. The challenges don't end here. In addition to confusion regarding various types of coaching, there is also the issue of determining what constitutes coaching in a given conversation. What managers often think of as coaching is not really coaching at all, especially from the salesperson's perspective. A more practical definition of sales coaching is useful so that we can clearly identify when we are coaching and when we are not.

INSPECTION DISGUISED
AS COACHING

A particularly subtle, and often overlooked, barrier to effective coaching concerns the nature of the coaching conversation and how it unfolds. We've said time and time again that sellers and managers have vastly different perceptions regarding the quantity and quality of the sales coaching taking place. We've listened to hundreds of coaching conversations over the years, and we introduce the following definitions and distinctions as an additional filter by which to judge the effectiveness of any given coaching conversation.

We can all agree that effective sales coaching helps prepare sellers to do something well, whether that is to expand large accounts, better allocate effort in a territory, properly qualify an opportunity, or conduct an effective sales call. Sales coaching is equipping salespeople to execute activities consistently well. The best sales coaching involves collaborative dialogue between manager and seller about the activities necessary to get that salesperson to quota. Valuable sales coaching is relevant, timely, and helpful to the seller.

> Sales coaching is equipping salespeople to execute activities consistently well.

Inspection, on the other hand, is about gathering information. Part of the reason managers inspect is to ensure that salespeople do things, but inspection alone doesn't allow managers to determine whether the things salespeople do are done *well*. Inspection is a forensic examination of what happened in the past. Inspection is a necessary activity for sales managers and often forms the basis for coaching; however, it is not the same thing as coaching. Many times, inspection feels irrelevant and unhelpful to salespeople, and as far as they are concerned, there's hardly ever a good time for it.

> Inspection is a forensic examination of
> what happened in the past.

We offer the following dialogue between our sales manager Nick and Sarah, one of the salespeople on his team. Nick looks forward to these calls because he gets the information that is required by his boss. While tedious, he recognizes that this is his chance to stay on top of what is happening. He believes that doing this will help Sarah stay focused on delivering her numbers.

EXAMPLE

Coaching Conversation 1

Nick: Sarah, it appears that your revenue performance is 20 percent behind plan for the first three months of the year.

Sarah: Yes, I know. I'm not happy about it.

Nick: Why do you think the numbers are so far off the mark?

Sarah: Well, I think the economy is affecting my customers' decisions. Many of their projects have been delayed.

Nick: Well, how many sales calls did you conduct last week?

Sarah: I went on 10 sales calls.

Nick: Your target is 16 per week. What happened?

Sarah: I had customer service issues to resolve. I spent one full day trying to resolve a billing issue for one of my customers.

Nick: Well, you are still responsible for making the targeted number of calls. You will need to find a way to hit your target.

Sarah: Well, perhaps you could help resolve some of the issues as they arise so I can free up more of my time.

Nick: I'll do what I can, but let's talk about your activity levels. How many appointments do you have set for next week?

Sarah: I have 9 scheduled calls, and I hope to set a few more.

Nick: I want to see that number at 16 meetings. Do whatever you need to do to increase the number of meetings. You can't hit your number if you aren't getting enough meetings.

Sarah: I know. I've just been bogged down with customer service issues.

Nick: Well, let's look at how you can increase your activity levels. How about if you and I meet for one hour each Friday to discuss your planned meetings for the following week? I believe the additional accountability will incent you to schedule more meetings. What do you think?

Sarah: Well, I'm already pressed for time. I'd prefer not to have more internal meetings, but I see your point. Maybe if I know that we will be discussing my call activities each Friday, I'll be more committed to getting my 16 meetings.

Nick: Let's meet each Friday at 8 a.m. to discuss your activities for the following week until you consistently hit your target number of meetings.

Sarah: OK.

DEBRIEF

If you are a sales manager, that conversation probably sounds somewhat typical. We hear conversations like this all the time. Nick found the dialogue useful because he felt like he was helping Sarah get on track to hit her target. Sarah found the dialogue useless because Nick created little value during the interaction. It was simply an inspection of her activity levels. Nick offered little in the way of guidance or real help to Sarah and left her feeling burdened with additional internal meetings.

Neil Rackham, an undisputed guru in the sales arena, proposed that a sales call was valuable only if the customer would have written the salesperson a check at the end of the meeting.* That *value* is something that a customer is willing to pay for. If we extend that idea to

---

* Neil Rackham and John R. DeVincentis, *Rethinking the Sales Force*, McGraw-Hill, New York, 1999.

coaching conversations between sales managers and the salespeople they manage, how many times would the salespeople be willing to pay for the coaching they received? Certainly not in the above example. Let's contrast this first example with a more extensive dialogue between Nick and Sarah and determine how this approach differs from the inspection-driven discussion.

EXAMPLE:

Coaching Conversation 2

Nick: Sarah, it appears that your revenue performance is 20 percent behind plan for the first three months of the year.

Sarah: Yes, I know. I'm not happy about it.

Nick: Why do you think the numbers are so far off the mark?

Sarah: Well, I think the economy is affecting my customers' decisions. Many of their projects have been delayed.

Nick: What about your activity levels. How many meetings have you been averaging per week?

Sarah: About 10.

Nick: Well, that is well below your target of 16 meetings per week. We will need to discuss how best to get you to your target. Meanwhile, let's examine the meetings you've been having and why many of your projects are delayed.

Sarah: OK, sounds good.

Nick: Let's take a look at whom you have been targeting. I see that the majority of your sales calls have been on current customers with the strategy of upgrading some of their current solutions to newer products. Has that been your intention?

Sarah: Yes, I've typically had more success upgrading current customers than going after new business.

Nick: How about the competitive trade-in promotions we have for some of our products—like baffles and ceiling tiles? Which competitor has the most market share of these products in your territory?

Sarah: It has to be Relianz. They sell the lower end of each of these products, typically to the smaller businesses.

Nick: I wonder if it might be more effective to target Relianz customers and offer the trade-in incentives. What are your thoughts on that?

Sarah: Well, I have quite a large base of Relianz customers in my territory. I know who they are. I actually had some success with one of these accounts last month. I traded in some of their drop ceilings for our acoustic ceiling tiles, and the trade-in value we provided was pretty impressive.

Nick: How many drop ceilings would you need to replace in the next three months to make up the 20 percent shortfall in revenue?

Sarah: The ceiling I replaced was $40,000 in revenue. I would have to sell eight of them in the next three months to hit my current quota and make up the shortfall, based on the current deals in my pipeline.

Nick: Think about the current customers you've had the most success with. Are they in a particular industry?

Sarah: Yes, actually, the older hotels and sports centers seem to be the most receptive to upgrading. The hotels typically have events happening simultaneously on multiple floors. The noise diminishes the client experience, and they lose repeat business as a result. The sports facilities have a similar problem with games happening on multiple floors.

Nick: So, would it make sense to narrow your focus to these two target groups that have good potential?

Sarah: That makes sense.

Nick: All right, what changes can you make to refocus your sales efforts to target those two groups?

Sarah: Well, I could spend half my time calling on Relianz customers about our upgrade promotions and the other half calling on my hotel and sports center customers.

Nick: I like that idea. What else can you do?

Sarah: I need to figure out what to say to get an appointment. I should come up with something that matters to each group of customers and something that demonstrates I understand their issues. If I can develop some compelling messaging, it may help me increase the number of meetings I'm able to get.

Nick: I agree. That's a good start. I suggest you make a list of the Relianz accounts as well as your hotel and sports center customers. Then jot down a few items you think would resonate with each group. We can review the target list and the concerns you think we can address. Let's get together again on Friday morning at 8 a.m.

Sarah: Sure, I'll have my list and ideas about what to say to them by Friday.

Nick: Sounds good. See you Friday.

DEBRIEF

Although this second dialogue included an element of inspection, Nick was much more deliberate in helping Sarah diagnose why the revenue target wasn't being achieved. In this second example, Nick helped Sarah shift her focus from calling exclusively on current customers to calling on a specific competitive base. He was also able to shift her current customer focus to a more clearly defined segment of hotels and sports centers. Sarah walked away from this conversation with a better understanding of how to improve. She obtained specific, actionable guidance that she could execute immediately.

That example of coaching dialogue illustrates how to use inspection as a pivot point for meaningful coaching. Our research has been very clear that high-performing managers are more likely to use scheduled time for coaching over inspection. More specifically, the bottom 25 percent of revenue-producing managers in our study were significantly more likely to use one-on-one coaching to inspect *prior* sales activity. Contrast that with the top 25 percent of revenue-producing managers who focus on helping salespeople prepare for *upcoming* activities. Figure 3.2 shows the comparison between the percentage of top performers who use scheduled time to inspect versus the percentage of their lower-performing peers who use scheduled time to inspect.

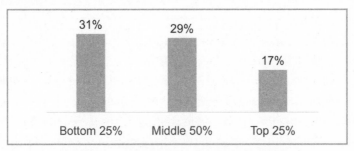

FIGURE 3.2 Inspection-Focused Interactions

Although coaching and inspection may not feel very different from the manager's perspective, they feel remarkably different to the salesperson. Inspection doesn't feel helpful, but coaching does. Inspection is often mandatory, whereas coaching is discretionary. An understanding of both coaching and inspection can help managers better recognize which conversations are valuable and which ones aren't. Awareness is often the first step in improving coaching efforts.

THE CURSE OF KNOWLEDGE: YOUR BIGGEST BLIND SPOT

It is probably safe to say that since managers are human, they have blind spots. We all do. So, what's the big deal? The curse of knowledge happens because once we know something (like how to sell against a thorny competitor), we don't remember what it was like *not to know it*. We assume that others (namely, our salespeople) have a similar frame of reference. This curse of knowledge causes us to be unintentionally unclear and ambiguous when providing direction to our salespeople. We often leave out crucial details that could have been helpful. We tell only part of the story, when we should have told the *whole* story. This leads to coaching short-hand. How bad is this curse of knowledge? What damage can it cause?

> The curse of knowledge causes us to be unintentionally
> unclear and ambiguous when providing direction
> to our salespeople. It is an error of omission.

Let's take a common example. You ask your sellers to complete a pre-call plan for all important sales calls. This is a very common expectation and yet one that is often poorly executed. You know that pre-call planning leads to better sales calls and better outcomes. Your salespeople know this too. The variance is *your* understanding versus *their* understanding of two key pieces of information. First, what constitutes a pre-call plan? Second, which sales calls are the important ones? This may seem like a very basic example; however, when we drill down a bit further, we see where the problems arise.

Let's start with the first question, "What constitutes a good pre-call plan?" As the sales manager, you may have a very clear vision that an effective pre-call plan includes the following items:

- An objective for the call

- An agenda with timings

- Key questions the seller should ask

- Possible solutions to discuss

- An actionable next step

When you review your seller's pre-call plan, you confront the following information:

- Background on the company

- LinkedIn information on the prospect

- Call objective

- A summary of prior conversations

Although this information is relevant, the seller is missing a few very important details. The seller's focus is more about what has been learned thus far. The manager's focus is about how to make progress in the next conversation. This variance in these two approaches could have been eliminated if the manager had clearly communicated (and reinforced through coaching) the expected content of an effective pre-call plan.

And how about what constitutes an important sales call? You might feel that any sales call on an opportunity of a given size constitutes an important sales call. Your salesperson may feel that only sales calls late in the sales cycle constitute important calls. Regardless of the reason for the disconnect, the manager and the seller are not on the same page. The curse of knowledge is an error of omission.

THE CULTURE OF DEPENDENCE: YOUR WORST ENEMY

This next barrier, unhealthy dependence, is dangerous and potentially crippling for sales managers. As managers, we want to be helpful. We want to add value. Sometimes we don't get this right. Sometimes we unintentionally get it wrong. Actions we take as managers that feel helpful in the moment can turn out to be hurtful in the long term. Let me explain.

Dependence is not inherently bad. It is the *level* of dependence that often goes awry. It is appropriate for salespeople to have some level of dependence on their sales manager. It is when this dependence becomes unhealthy that problems arise. Unhealthy dependence on the sales manager often occurs because of a lack of clarity between the role of the manager and the role of the seller. The roles become blurred. This blurring of roles contributes to a chronic case of overworked, overwhelmed sales managers. Many sales managers are not clear in their own mind about what constitutes their job versus the job of their salespeople. This is particularly acute for (but certainly not limited to) newly promoted sales managers. As always, a real-life example is useful to make this point.

> Unhealthy dependence on the sales manager often occurs because a lack of clarity between the role of the manager and the role of the salesperson. The roles become blurred.

In one of our sales management workshops, we were discussing the issue of prioritization and boundary setting. One newly promoted sales manager emphatically shared that he was *always available* and answered his phone whenever one of his salespeople called. When I questioned him further, he admitted that there were indeed a few types of situations where he didn't answer the phone—such as when he was attending a sales call. However, he was truly on call most of the time. He was also very stressed.

While the new and stressed-out sales manager was proudly sharing his story of constant availability, a grizzled veteran sales manager said, "Harrumph! I never answer my phone!"

Aghast, the newly promoted sales manager said, "How can you do that! It's your job to help your team. What if they need you and can't get ahold of you?"

To that, the grizzled veteran replied, "I have a policy that I wait one hour before responding. I listen to the voice mail, and if it is truly urgent, I respond sooner. If it is not urgent, I wait the allotted hour. You would be amazed at the number of times the problem is resolved within that hour."

This may seem like an example of extremes. It isn't. The difference between the newly promoted sales manager and the experienced sales manager was mindset. The new manager felt responsible for everything. The experienced sales manager knew that he couldn't possibly do everything. Experienced sales managers know that they must equip their team to do *their* jobs effectively. How do you know whether you've created unhealthy dependence with your team? How do you know if you have the right mindset? Well, you've probably identified with the plight of some of the sales managers we've discussed. If you'd like to take a short quiz to get a better handle on how dependence affects your management results, please visit our website at www.vantagepointperformance.com/crushingquota.

THE BEST PATH FORWARD

The first order of business is to establish a common language. We need to be very clear what we mean by *sales coaching* as compared to *other* types of coaching we do as sales managers. We need to put a stake in the ground and agree on what sales coaching is and how it fits into the way we interact with our salespeople. A common language helps managers and salespeople get on the same page. It reduces the prevalent disconnects between manager and seller perception. It forms the foundation for effective coaching.

Although having a common coaching language is the first order of business, sales managers also need a way to decide what to coach. Knowing what sales coaching is matters, and knowing what kind of coaching to do matters even more. Managers need to coach what they can affect. Our research has revealed that the only things managers can directly manage are sales activities. Sales coaching should be tied to sales activities. Which activities? Why? How do managers decide? Sales coaching is more science than art. Managers need a way to examine a seller's role and use that information to provide the type of coaching that will get that seller to quota.

Finally, sales managers need to ensure that the coaching they provide is helpful and valuable to the salespeople they manage. They need to do more coaching and less inspection. They need to build healthy boundaries with the salespeople they manage in order to build highly functioning teams. The next chapter paves the way for effective sales coaching by establishing a common language for coaching—one that ensures that coaching efforts are most likely to lead to better sales performance. It is time to remove the guesswork and apply some science to sales coaching.

PART II

THE GROUNDWORK FOR GREATNESS

CHAPTER 4

DECIDING WHAT
TO COACH

We have spent some time in the preceding three chapters examining what sales coaching is *not*, and we've explored many of the reasons effective coaching is not common practice. We've examined the situational factors that impede coaching. We've explored the challenges managers have in shifting their mindset from superstar salesperson to sales manager.

We've done this examination to get you into a mindset that allows you to receive the information we share in this chapter and the ones that follow. In this chapter, we take the first step in establishing a common language for sales coaching. We use powerful research findings to unpack the nature of sales coaching and how to select the best type of sales coaching for your sales team. If this feels hopeful, good. It is. Read on.

THE COACHING CHASM

Let's start by reflecting on the reasons we coach our salespeople. Why do we coach? Well, of course we coach to help our sellers reach their quotas. To reach our company's revenue targets. We coach so that we can achieve the outcomes we want. This reasoning, sound as it is, creates what we refer to as the *coaching chasm*. We coach because we want certain outcomes, but we can't coach those outcomes *directly*. The outcomes we want are the culmination of many things we do as organizations, managers, and salespeople. We can coach only to things that *lead to* quota and revenue attainment. We cannot coach to the outcomes themselves.

The chasm lies in the reality that although we coach our sellers to achieve certain outcomes—like quota attainment—the outcomes themselves don't respond to coaching. We'd like to find the sales manager who had success coaching her sellers by saying, "Go make quota. Go get more revenue." Yes, this chasm between the outcomes we want and coaching that is truly helpful is real. Even the most successful sales managers fall into the trap of coaching in ways that are not directly executable. To illustrate this point, I'll share a true and oddly amusing story about a sales manager named Glen.

Glen was a superstar sales manager, and we met him while working with the sales leadership team of a major healthcare company. We loved Glen. He was charismatic, dedicated, and open to new ideas on how best to manage his sales team. We wish our workshops were full of folks like Glen.

During a sales leadership workshop, we had just concluded a discussion about the importance of coaching to sales activities. We contrasted how much more helpful it is to a salesperson when we focus our coaching efforts on the things they do, day in and day out, rather than focusing on the outcomes we hold them accountable to achieve. It was a discussion about how to make our coaching actionable to the salespeople we coach.

At that point in the meeting, Glen looked somewhat uncomfortable. That was unusual for Glen because he had been highly involved throughout the workshop. We asked him what was wrong. At first, he seemed hesitant to respond, but then he proceeded to candidly share an aha moment. He said that he had just realized that he had been making a major mistake in his initial conversations with his new-hire salespeople. Glen proceeded to tell us that whenever a new salesperson had joined his team, he would always get some version of the question, "What do you expect of me?" His go-to answer for this very important question had been, "I expect you to make your number." Well, clearly that was true. That is certainly a reasonable expectation. It just isn't very helpful.

Everyone in sales knows that quota attainment is king. However, what Glen realized at that moment was that his salespeople were really asking a different question. Instead of, "What do you expect of me?" what they were really asking was, "In order to succeed here, what do we need to do?" This is a very different, yet relevant question. This is the question that the most successful sales managers answer for their salespeople. And when they provide this level of clarity, more of their salespeople succeed. It stands to reason that more salespeople would make quota if they just knew how.

CLARITY OF TASK:
YOUR SALESPERSON'S BEST FRIEND

As leaders, we are often lulled into the mistaken notion that money is all that matters to salespeople. The more money salespeople have an opportunity to make, the more motivated they will become. Leaders spend millions of dollars devising the perfect compensation plan to drive the desired sales behaviors. This is not all bad. Compensation matters, just not as much as we might believe.

Stephen Doyle and Ben Shapiro were keenly interested to learn just how important compensation was in motivating salesperson behavior.* They wanted to challenge the conventional wisdom and find out if there

---

* Stephen X. Doyle and Benson P. Shapiro, "What Counts Most in Motivating Your Sales Force," *Harvard Business Review*, July 1980.

were other, more important factors in play. These researchers examined factors that were most likely to influence salesperson motivation, and they determined the relative influence of each factor. As it turned out, there were only three things that mattered regarding seller motivation, and they are shown in Figure 4.1. *Incentive compensation, need for achievement,* and *clarity of the sales task* were the only three things that significantly influenced salesperson motivation. Of those three factors, clarity of the sales task was by far the most powerful predictor of motivation. In fact, clarity of the sales task accounted for more than *three times* the variance in salesperson motivation compared with incentive compensation.

Motivating Factor	Percent of Variation Explained by Factor
Clarity of the sales task	33.6
Need for achievement	21.2
Incentive compensation	11.6

FIGURE 4.1 **The Relative Strength of Three Factors in Motivating Salespeople**
Source: Adapted from Stephen X. Doyle and Benson P. Shapiro, "What Counts Most in Motivating Your Sales Force," Harvard Business Review, July 1980.

Since task clarity plays such a significant role in salesperson motivation, it's useful to understand what it means. *Clarity of task* is the degree to which the activities you ask sellers to perform are directly aligned with the results they are held accountable to achieve.

> **Clarity of task:** The degree to which the activities you ask sellers to perform are directly aligned with the results they are held accountable to achieve.

The surprising findings by Doyle and Shapiro, published in their *Harvard Business Review* article, were counter to conventional wisdom; however, they make sense when we examine real-life sales jobs, and we can see especially why task clarity is so significant. Let's compare two separate sales situations to make this point more tangible. Both sales situations described were real, and they were positions actually held by one highly tenured, very successful salesperson.

In the first situation, the salesperson was selling assessment services for a very well established assessment company. This company had a validated sales assessment instrument that was very credible in the industry. In this role, the salesperson sold both individual salesperson assessments for recruitment and hiring purposes, as well as broader audits of sales talent across a sales organization. The product was well defined: the target audience for the individual assessment was human resources, and the target audience for the talent audit was sales leadership. The compensation plan was a straight percentage of revenue generated. In this situation, the salesperson exceeded revenue targets consistently over a four-year period.

In that first sales situation, the sellers' task was clear: sell two products to two well-defined audiences. No ambiguity. No reason to lose focus or be confused. That was important because ambiguity is a motivation and productivity killer. However, is it possible to take a highly talented salesperson and cause him or her to fail unintentionally? You bet.

Fast-forward to the second situation. This same highly successful salesperson left to take on a new and exciting role. An established training company was embarking on a new line of business. The company wanted to get into the assessment business. The company's leaders had several ideas about viable instruments, but the company was relatively new to the assessment space. This salesperson was hired because he knew the industry and he had proven success in selling assessment services. However, the assessment solution was more of an idea than a reality. The prevailing idea shared by the company's leaders was, "You sell it, and we will build it." The compensation plan was far richer for this solution, and it included an accelerator that kicked in after the first major sale. Income potential was unlimited.

The company's leaders were confident that if they got enough good people together, those people would figure it out. Well, that didn't happen. This previously successful salesperson failed in this role. He tried to figure it out but couldn't. As he experienced multiple failed attempts to sell this "idea" to prospective clients, his frustration grew. After about 18 months, he left the company. He no longer cared about unlimited income potential. He wanted to sell something. He wanted to have something to sell that prospects wanted to buy. He wanted clarity of task, and he didn't have it. He left when he couldn't figure out how to succeed.

If your sellers have a clear task before them, they will succeed. If their task is murky, they will fumble and fail. Your job as a coach is to provide that clarity of task.

THE RELATIONSHIP BETWEEN COACHING AND QUOTA ATTAINMENT

Shapiro and Doyle's findings support the link between the clarity of the sales task and motivation and demonstrate the importance of identifying which activities matter. As sales managers, we care about seller motivation. But we care even more about results. About quota achievement. We want evidence that focusing on activities leads to better performance.

Although it makes intuitive sense that coaching to activities is important, it helps to know just how much this matters. How does coaching to activities compare with other types of coaching we provide to our sellers? Ultimately, we want evidence that coaching this way is more effective than coaching in other ways. In other words, the question we want to answer is, which type of coaching really leads to better salesperson performance? This is a question that I (Michelle) have been incredibly curious about, and I have spent the last four years answering it.

I set out to determine which of the most common types of management attention and coaching mattered the most with regard to quota attainment. I gathered details regarding the types of coaching salespeople received from their managers and the degree to which this coaching was correlated with higher levels of salesperson performance.

I asked salespeople to rate the degree to which their managers focused on the (1) the results they were held accountable to achieve (revenue, volume, and so on); (2) their capabilities (skills and abilities); and (3) the activities in which the seller engaged (making sales calls, conducting product demos, and so on). I chose these three aspects of coaching because they are the most prevalent, and they receive the most attention from leadership. My findings on the impact of these three aspects of coaching on quota attainment are provided in Figure 4.2.

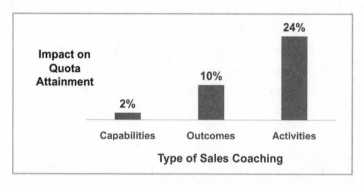

FIGURE 4.2 Comparison of the Results of Three Types of Coaching
Source: Vantage Point Sales Management Survey, Vantage Point Performance, Inc.
Note: n = 518.

As with most of the research studies we've conducted, we gained some interesting insights, but they were not necessarily the ones we thought we would see. Like everyone else who has had a career in sales, I had bought into the conventional wisdom that coaching was *primarily* intended to build seller capability. I fully expected that coaching to seller capabilities would be strongly correlated to quota attainment. It wasn't. In fact, the relationship between coaching to seller capabilities and quota attainment was the weakest of the three types of coaching. Who knew?

I also expected (based on the findings of plenty of other studies) that attention to results would be *strongly* correlated with quota attainment. In fact, the link between attention to results and higher sales performance was the *only* consistent finding in prior studies. Well, I did not find a strong relationship between attention to results and higher quota attainment. Nothing of significance.

It turned out that coaching to *activities* was the only type of coaching significantly related to quota attainment. We knew this intuitively, but now we had evidence. Over 20 percent of the variance in quota attainment was attributed to activity coaching, providing additional support for the need for clarity of task. Neither coaching to results nor coaching to capabilities reached significance in the analysis. Hmmm. Interesting. How could this be?

> Coaching to activities was the only type of coaching significantly related to performance, and it accounted for over 20 percent of the variance in quota attainment.

Why Our Findings Were Unique

Why did so many other studies find a link between management attention to results and improved sales performance, but we did not? Why were we the first researchers to find this powerful relationship between attention to activities and sales performance?

Upon further examination, it is likely that the results of many prior studies are misleading. Many researchers use a self-report measure for seller performance. In other words, they ask sellers how well they *feel* they perform *relative* to their peers. It is human nature to overestimate your performance. We all have very high opinions of ourselves. When asked, we typically feel that we are, worst case, at least slightly better than our peers.

For example, if you ask people who drive how they rate their driving ability, they will most likely report that they are better than 75 percent of the drivers on the road. Almost everyone says this. How can the majority of drivers on the road be in the top 25 percent of drivers? They're not. They just think they are. The same is true of salespeople. Ask them a subjective question, and you will get a subjective answer.

So, how big a role does subjectivity play in research findings? Why should we care? Because the way we measure sales performance matters. In my study, I also gathered a self-report measure of performance. And when I analyzed the data using the self-report measure, I had findings similar to those of prior studies. I could have stopped there and just been happy with my confirmatory findings.

However, when I analyzed the self-report measure, *all three types of coaching* were significantly correlated to sales performance. Yep, all three types of coaching—results, capabilities, and activities—were positively and strongly correlated with sales performance. Or, more accurately, salespeople's *perceptions* of their performance.

These findings are interesting and consistent with prior studies, but they are not practically useful. As sales managers, we coach our salespeople so that they can make quota. We want our salespeople to feel good about themselves; however, that's not enough to hit our revenue targets. As sales managers, we need to know how to get our sellers to quota, and that is the measure by which our coaching should be evaluated. When quota attainment is the important measure of performance—which it is in every sales organization—then coaching to activities is the only way to get there.

So, let's think about this. The research clearly reveals that the most important type of coaching is aimed at activities, not outcomes or capabilities. How have we missed this after more than a hundred years of professional sales management? Well, the answer lies in the old saying, "The squeaky wheel gets the grease." The biggest squeak we hear from the sales force is the missed revenue targets. Results, not activities.

If activities are so important, how prevalent is activity management? How much attention do organizations pay to the management of activities? The answer may surprise you. Do organizations track, manage, and report what matters most to the targets they are looking to hit? As it turns out, they don't.

WHAT'S MEASURED VERSUS WHAT'S MANAGEABLE

It is useful to examine just how sales activities fit within the scheme of overall salesperson performance and the way that performance is measured. In our book *Cracking the Sales Management Code*, we shared the results of a three-year study into the metrics sales organizations use to measure individual and organizational sales performance. These metrics were the things organizations cared about. Since these were the rulers by which sales success was measured, they certainly deserved a closer look.

We wanted to know what we could we learn from these measurement practices and the practical implications for sales management. We wanted to know how these metrics related to sales coaching. After all, this was a book about sales coaching. Our research highlighted why much of what's measured, and the associated reports managers receive, does not directly assist their coaching efforts.

In our study, we revealed three distinct levels of sales metrics that were tracked and reported. These three levels of metrics were not readily apparent, and it took a tremendous amount of due diligence to devise our framework. The good news is that once the framework emerged, it became a powerful tool for managers to use to determine how data can inform better sales coaching.

The first, or highest, level of metrics are business results. *Business results* are organizational targets or outcomes that are used to measure the health of the organization. Business results are not directly manageable because they are outcomes of seller effort. Examples of business results are provided below:

Business Results

- Revenue

- Profit

- Market share

The next level of metrics are sales objectives. *Sales objectives* are interim guideposts, or key performance indicators, that organizations establish to provide directional guidance for seller effort. Sales objectives are not directly manageable; however, they can be strongly influenced by sales managers. Examples of sales objectives are provided below:

Sales Objectives

- Product penetration per account

- Sales by customer type

- Close rate

The third and final level of metrics in our framework are sales activities. *Sales activities* are things sellers do to make sales. Sales activities are directly manageable, and they form the fodder for the most effective sales coaching. Some examples are provided below:

Sales Activities

- Product demonstrations conducted

- Proposals delivered

- Call plan usage

.   .   .

We will devote the majority of the rest of this book to the coaching of activities, but first we let's see how these three levels of metrics fit together:

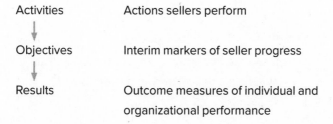

Salespeople execute sales activities (sales calls, demonstrations, account plans, and so on) to achieve specific sales objectives (sell certain products, sell to certain types of customers, improve close rates) to achieve desired results (quota, revenue, and volume targets). These interrelationships among activities, objectives, and results help sales managers provide clarity of task for their salespeople, which improves seller motivation and drives better sales performance. The research on the importance of sales activities is clear. However, this research is not reflected in the way organizations measure their sales force.

In our study of sales metrics, only 17 percent of the metrics we examined were sales activities. That means that a whopping 83 percent of the metrics organizations measure and report are not directly manageable. If something isn't manageable, it is most certainly not coachable. This supports our recent finding of a lack of correlation between management attention to results and improved sales performance. The bulk of what we measure does not lead to better sales performance, and it can't be directly coached. But the sad story gets more depressing.

Even within the 17 percent of metrics that fell into the activity category, most of those metrics did not relate directly to selling efforts. When all was said and done and the analysis was complete, only about 8 percent of the metrics in our study involved seller activities related to *making sales*. The other 9 percent of activity-level metrics involved the things organizations do to enable their sellers, such as training and performance assessment. So, in the end, our study revealed that the companies we studied applied only 8 percent of their measurement and reporting efforts to the things salespeople to do make more sales. Activities. The things that *are* strongly correlated to achieving quota.

> **Only 8 percent of the metrics in our study involved seller activities related to *making sales*.**

Activity *measurement* does not equate to activity *management*. Just measuring something does not necessarily make it better. When we studied management coaching efforts, the most successful managers *coached* to activities. They didn't just measure them. In the balance of this chapter, we explore the types of activities in which salespeople engage and how those activities are related, and then we provide a way to help managers determine which activities they *should* coach.

THE NATURE OF SALES ACTIVITIES

Chances are, you manage a certain type of team. You probably manage a group of salespeople with similar roles. You may manage inside sales representatives or territory salespeople, or perhaps you manage major account sales executives. In other words, you manage a team in which your salespeople have *similar job characteristics*. The characteristics of the salespeople's jobs dictate the types of activities in which they engage. Activities for each role do not occur in isolation. They occur in highly related ways—in groups. Understanding these groups of activities helps provide the context needed for robust and relevant sales coaching.

In our groundbreaking study of sales metrics, published in our book *Cracking the Sales Management Code,* we closely examined the types of activities in which salespeople engaged. We looked for patterns of sales activity, and we found some. It turns out that seller activities are not random, but instead, they cluster into like groups of a similar nature. We identified four distinct *groups* of activities in which salespeople engage. These groups of activities work together to drive specific types of sales *outcomes*. Because of this synergistic relationship within groups of activities, we can think of these groups of activities as processes. Four groups of activities, designed to produce four different outcomes, hence four *sales processes*. A brief description of each process is provided in Figure 4.3.

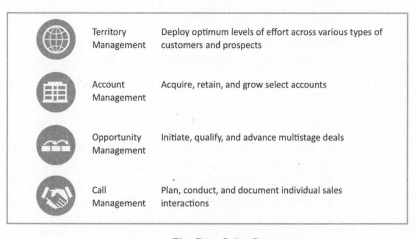

	Territory Management	Deploy optimum levels of effort across various types of customers and prospects
	Account Management	Acquire, retain, and grow select accounts
	Opportunity Management	Initiate, qualify, and advance multistage deals
	Call Management	Plan, conduct, and document individual sales interactions

FIGURE 4.3 The Four Sales Processes

The four sales processes and associated activities are separate and distinct. In Figure 4.4, we describe the conditions that indicate when each sales process is needed. These conditions reflect *the job characteristics* that relate to a salesperson's role. Some combination of the four sales processes will be relevant to each salesperson's role. This is also holds true for the salespeople you manage.

Sales Process		When Needed
	Territory Management	There are many customers and prospects, and they are not equally attractive. Prioritization is required to maximize sales efforts.
	Account Management	Select customers are vital to organization performance. Special, in-depth attention must be given to acquire, retain, or grow these important accounts.
	Opportunity Management	Individual deals are large and complex, and they involve multiple decision-makers. Competition is typically strong. Winning requires thoughtful strategy.
	Call Management	The outcome of a given sales interaction is important. Each interaction is unique and therefore requires advanced preparation.

FIGURE 4.4 Conditions That Indicate When Each Sales Process Is Needed

Territory Management Activities

As we indicated, territory management is warranted when a salesperson's assignment includes a large number of customers and prospects. There is no magic number of customers that define when territory management is useful. It is more a matter of the practical reality that the salesperson can't attend to them all equally. Nor should he or she. A territory doesn't have to be a terrestrial geography. It can be any set of assigned customers and prospects, whether that is a physical or virtual territory. So, for example, an inside salesperson's *territory* is her assigned list of people to call.

Figure 4.5 reflects a sample territory management process. Although the exact steps in a territory management process may be different from

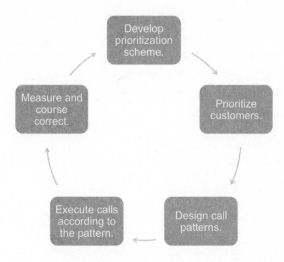

FIGURE 4.5 **Sample Territory Management Process**

organization to organization, all effective processes include these core elements: developing a prioritization scheme, prioritizing customers, designing call patterns according to the prioritization scheme, and executing calls accordingly. Progress is measured, and course corrections are made. As sales assignments change and territories are redefined, the process starts again.

Account Management Activities

Account management is necessary when a single account is large and important enough to warrant significant attention and effort. Whereas territory management concerns balancing effort across many accounts and prospects, account management efforts are aimed at a single customer. Figure 4.6 reflects a sample account management process.

Account management is a long-term proposition, with no beginning, middle, or end. Account management is iterative and continuous. Account management activities revolve around the development, execution, and continual refinement of account plans to help salespeople penetrate, retain, and grow large accounts.

FIGURE 4.6 Sample Account Management Process

The most important strategic activity within account management is the development of an account plan. The most effective plans reflect a keen understanding of the customer's needs, goals, and objectives, and they align potential solutions to customer needs to create mutual value. Once account strategies have been developed, action plans are crafted to ensure effective execution of the plan. Account progress is typically measured at predetermined intervals, and adjustments are made as needed to course correct. Adjustments are made, plans are refined, and the process repeats.

Opportunity Management Activities

Opportunity management is necessary when winning individual deals is complex, requires multiple interactions, and often involves multiple decision-makers. Opportunity management activities help salespeople uncover, qualify, pursue, and win individual deals. Opportunity management is portrayed as a linear set of activities because opportunities have a beginning, a middle, and an end. We either win a piece of business or we don't. Figure 4.7 reflects a sample opportunity management process.

FIGURE 4.7 **Sample Opportunity Management Process**

Activities in the early stage of opportunity pursuit are oriented toward understanding buyer needs and qualifying the opportunity. These early activities are necessary to help the salesperson determine if an opportunity is worthy of pursuit. Once a salesperson decides to pursue an opportunity, activities revolve around the identification and shaping of buying criteria. Solutions are developed and positioned to best differentiate the seller's solutions against competing alternatives. Terms are negotiated, concerns are addressed, and deals are won or lost.

Call Management Activities

Call management activities involve planning, conducting, and capturing individual customer interactions. Most call management processes are designed to help salespeople conduct more effective sales conversations. Call management is most important when individual customer interactions have a significant impact on the salesperson's likelihood of winning a sale. Figure 4.8 reflects a sample call management process.

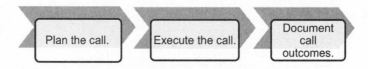

FIGURE 4.8 **Sample Call Management Process**

Salespeople conduct sales calls for many reasons. They make sales calls on customers and prospects to identify new opportunities, pursue and win opportunities, and retain existing business. The planning and execution of any given sales call is highly dependent upon the reason for the call. Most call management processes are designed to help salespeople plan and conduct sales calls in pursuit of individual opportunities.

SALES PROCESSES WORK TOGETHER

You can think of the four sales processes as working together. As indicated in Figure 4.9, territory and account management are two primary processes that salespeople employ to *create new opportunities*. Salespeople allocate planning effort and make a higher number of sales calls on high-potential customers within their territories to maximize territory penetration. Salespeople also exert planning effort and make sales calls on large accounts to increase share of wallet, expand their footprint, and generate additional revenue. Whether salespeople are mining a given territory or mining an individual large account, they are looking to get more business, typically in the form of new opportunities.

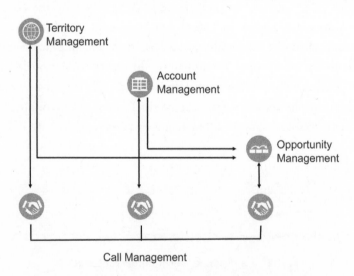

FIGURE 4.9 The Four Sales Processes Working Together

Opportunity and call management processes work together to help salespeople *win business* they've identified. Opportunity management processes are designed to help salespeople strategize and navigate multiple stages of the sales cycle to qualify, compete, and win. Call management helps salespeople plan for and navigate individual sales calls within opportunity pursuit. So, salespeople make calls to generate opportunities within their accounts and territories, as well as to pursue opportunities they've generated. As illustrated in Figure 4.9, call management is the underpinning and primary means of execution for all sales processes.

MATCHING SALES ROLES AND SALES PROCESSES

When you consider the wide range of activities you *could* coach, which ones *should* you coach? This is an important question and one that we will begin to tackle in this section. To determine which type of coaching you should provide, it is useful to revisit the nature of the roles of the salespeople you manage and determine which sales processes are aligned with those roles. Should you be doing territory coaching, account coaching, opportunity coaching, or call coaching? How do you decide? It is likely that more than one sales process is relevant to the salespeople on your team and that they would benefit from some combination of coaching.

The most effective way to make this salesperson role and sales process connection is to explore a real example. Within your organization, you may have only one sales role, or you may have many sales roles. Regardless of the complexity of your sales organization, examination of the roles you manage will help you determine the most relevant type of coaching.

EXAMPLE

Client Manager for Financial Services Company

Individuals in this role are responsible for managing up to 15 existing client relationships. Current client contracts are up for renewal once per year. Each contract is large and includes a financial risk strategy for the client. Sellers are responsible for retaining existing clients and expanding the size and scope of client contracts. It is not possible for client managers to achieve quota exclusively through contract renewal. Average revenue targets are in the $10 million range, including renewals and account expansion.

Client managers expand existing relationships by identifying additional risk mitigation opportunities within the client organizations they manage. Each year, client managers receive comprehensive data regarding the client's contract usage.

They analyze the data to determine areas for possible expansion. They can accomplish account growth via expansion into additional business units and/or expanding the existing portfolio within each business unit. In addition to the client manager, each account has a contract administrator to deal with the day-to-day administration of their contract.

RELEVANT SALES PROCESSES

Account management is highly relevant for the client manager. Due to the size and scope of client contracts, each account represents a significant portion of the seller's total revenue target. Because quota attainment requires account expansion, new opportunities must be uncovered. The development of a comprehensive account plan, including analysis of data to identify expansion opportunities, is a crucial part of account management.

Opportunity management is also highly relevant to the client manager. Once areas for growth are identified, client managers must qualify and pursue these opportunities to expand the size and scope of client contracts. Individual opportunities may include a variety of different client contacts, possibly residing in multiple business units.

Call management is relevant for the client managers because they have to make calls to identify new opportunities. In the case of the client manager, very thorough account expansion strategies have been developed using account data. Client managers must be very deliberate and strategic in how they plan and conduct sales calls to explore these expansion areas. These calls are a vital precursor for opportunity generation, and if they are ineffective, no opportunities will result.

Territory management is not relevant to the client manager role because each salesperson only has 15 or fewer accounts. All accounts must be attended to, and they all have potential for either expansion or retention. Prioritizing which accounts to manage would be a waste of time. In most instances, either territory management *or* account management will be relevant, but not both. Salespeople either tend to have a small number of large accounts or a large number of small to midsize accounts.

In the case of this client manager, three sales processes were relevant. Each of the three sales processes had multiple associated activities. This was true for the client manager in our financial services client, and it is probably true for the salespeople you manage. As a sales manager, clarifying what your sellers should be doing is important; however, *all* relevant activities don't necessarily provide fodder for the *best* coaching opportunities.

SELECTING ACTIVITIES THAT MATTER MOST

Up to this point, we've provided evidence that coaching to activities is the *only* type of coaching significantly related to quota attainment. We shared research regarding the types of activities salespeople execute that could warrant coaching. We explored the way activities work together in groups, or processes, to achieve specific outcomes. We've even provided examples of how different sales processes apply to a given sales role. Ultimately, however, effective coaching must target *individual activities*.

You are probably already of the mind that not all sales activities are equally important. As a sales manager, you probably have a well-developed sense for how sellers should apply their effort. Our goal is to provide a research-based prioritization approach that, if applied consistently, will lead you to the right answer every time. We use all three levels of metrics in this approach because all three levels are necessary to create the best path to results for each of your salespeople and increase the likelihood of making quota. As a sales manager, it is *your job* to connect the dots between these three levels of metrics to ensure that salespeople focus their effort on the right things. So, how do you connect these dots? How do you use the three levels as a framework for better decision-making? The key is to begin with the outcome and work your way backward. Figure 4.10 illustrates how this important task unfolds.

As a sales manager, you probably have a well-developed sense for how sellers should apply their effort. Our goal is to provide a research-based prioritization approach that, if applied consistently, will lead you to the right answer every time.

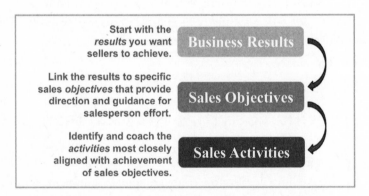

FIGURE 4.10 Task 1. Identify the Coachable *Activities*

Let's continue with our financial services example. This client was well established and had been a market leader for approximately 50 years. The company employed very smart people and was excellent at customer service. However, over time, growth had slowed. This was particularly problematic because at the time they engaged with us, they had growth targets in the double digits for the next five years.

When we looked deeper into the organization to better understand what was happening, we got a clearer picture of the reasons for their lack of growth within existing clients. The client managers, responsible for selling to an existing account base, were not really selling. They were very smart customer service representatives. They had many certifications in the financial industry, and they were heralded as experts in their field.

However, as most of us are keenly aware, selling involves more than the sharing of expertise. In this case, selling required dedicated planning and execution of those plans to uncover new needs. Selling required expansion into other areas of their customer base and proactively identifying areas for growth. Selling required that client managers manage client engagements in a fundamentally *different* way. This is what our client needed for these client managers to be doing, and it wasn't happening.

The good news was that this client had a very large customer base. The bad news was that this base was stagnant. Account expansion was not happening. It was clear that their client managers had to behave more like sellers and less like customer service representatives to turn this around. They would have to do things differently.

This required a major shift in focus. This sort of shift can seem daunting unless you have a way to narrow down the size of the change into something manageable. The example in Figure 4.11 illustrates how this results, objectives, and activities framework helped them orient their client

FIGURE 4.11 Task 1. Identify the Coachable *Activities* for Our Financial Services Client

managers toward the activities that had the greatest impact. These activities were the most likely to grow their currently stagnant, but potentially lucrative, account base.

This client had developed a comprehensive method for analyzing client data within each account to identify possible areas for contract expansion. This was an important part of the company's overall account management process. In addition, they had developed and documented a structure for engaging key contacts, within each account, in a formal meeting to explore areas for contract expansion. The processes for account analysis (account management) and engagement in formal meetings (call management) were thorough, well documented, and effective. Unfortunately, they weren't being used. The client managers viewed both activities as optional, and they had opted out. In this situation, as in many of our client situations, deploying a new process would not necessarily lead to adoption of that process. This client needed to employ standards to further clarify expectations for how activities within that process would be executed.

STANDARDS AS CONTRIBUTORS TO CLARITY OF TASK

Standards are specific guidelines, or expectations, that if met will lead to effective and consistent execution of sales activities. Oftentimes our clients feel that telling sellers *what* to do is enough to ensure compliance. We have found that telling salespeople *what* to do is often not enough. All too frequently, ambiguity still exists regarding the execution of a particular activity. In the case of this client example, recall the first critical activity as reflected in Figure 4.12.

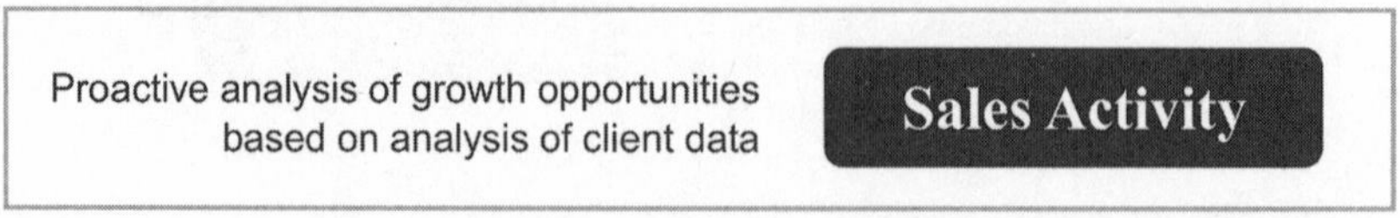

FIGURE 4.12 **First Critical Activity for Our Financial Services Client**

Regarding this proactive analysis, we found that although the client managers were getting data, they were unclear on how to tie the data to specific solution recommendations to expand the product set. Training and associated documentation were provided to equip these sellers to conduct this important analysis and develop relevant recommendations. The training and associated documentation answered the questions, "How do I do this well? How do I use the data to conduct an effective account analysis?"

It doesn't matter how much of an activity salespeople perform if they are not executing the activity correctly. In order for the execution of activities to lead to the objectives we've identified, the activities must be executed well—to a standard of what constitutes success. The training and documentation our client company provided addressed the *qualitative* aspect of activity standards. The company trained the client managers on how to conduct the analysis correctly and how to develop meaningful recommendations for expansion.

In addition to equipping the sellers to enable them to conduct account analysis in the most effective way, sellers needed guidance on when or how much of this type of analysis to conduct. They needed *quantitative* standards. In this case, existing accounts over a certain recurring revenue threshold were identified as targets for the account analysis. This clarity of account targets removed any ambiguity regarding *which* accounts to analyze. This clarification answered the question, "*How much* (or how many) account analyses do we conduct in my assignment?" By creating absolute clarity regarding *how* to conduct the account analysis and *how many* analyses needed to be conducted, it was far easier to hold the client managers accountable for these vital activities. Clarity of task in action.

KEY TAKEAWAYS: THE BEGINNING OF A COMMON LANGUAGE FOR COACHING

We began this chapter by revealing the *coaching chasm:* the things you want to change through coaching are uncoachable. Although you want your salespeople to hit quota, and you want to hit certain volume and revenue targets, outcomes don't respond to coaching. You can coach only activities—not outcomes.

We also shared new research that reinforces that observation. If you're like us, these insights have forced you to rethink some of your own coaching behavior—just like Glen, reflecting on the misguided "coaching" that he had dispensed in the past. This all brings us to the questions this chapter was intended to answer: Of all the things we could coach, what should we coach? How do we go about answering that question as sales managers?

We introduced the notion of clarity of task—what it is and why it is the most important aspect of seller motivation. We provided evidence that sellers need, and benefit from knowing, the direct link between the activities you ask them to perform and the outcomes you are holding them accountable to achieve. We explored evidence that debunked the idea that salespeople are coin-operated. Income matters, but clarity matters more.

Because coaching to sales activities is the most productive fodder for coaching effort, we provided additional research about the nature of activities and how they occur within groups to drive specific types of sales outcomes. We introduced the four sales processes and examined the types of activities that occur within each one. We explored the way in which job characteristics of the salesperson's role dictate which sales processes are relevant.

We shared a research-based framework for creating clarity of task for your salespeople. We did this by connecting the dots between sales results, sales objectives, and sales activities. We left nothing to chance with our approach by introducing activity standards. We explored *qualitative standards* to ensure that sellers know how to execute activities effectively and *quantitative standards* to clarify when and how much of an activity is expected.

This chapter provided very specific guidance to help you determine what your sellers should be doing to reach quota. It also formed the basis of the fodder for your coaching efforts. In the following chapters, we will get even more detailed regarding the tactics needed to build rich coaching conversations, conduct them in the most effective way, and then determine how often to conduct the various types of coaching conversations. We leave no coaching stone unturned.

CHAPTER 5

STRUCTURING COACHING CONVERSATIONS

Hopefully by this point you are sufficiently motivated to coach. In the last chapter, we equipped you with a powerful way to determine *what* you should be coaching. We did that to ensure that your coaching is relevant and linked to what matters most to the salespeople you manage. Knowing what to coach is critical. Quite frankly, this is where most coaching models fail. If managers are not coaching the right things, it doesn't matter how well the coaching unfolds. It is like doing a masterful job of driving to the wrong destination. It doesn't matter how good of a driver you are if you end up in the wrong place.

We offered a very direct path to selecting the best activities to coach, to ensure that you are heading to the right destination. Now it is time to take the next step in your coaching journey. It is time to learn *how* to coach effectively. It is often said that the devil is in the details, and we agree. In this chapter, we share the details that lead to good coaching. The details that, when implemented, will help you get more of your sellers to quota.

If you are committed to spending time coaching your salespeople, it pays to get it right. We mean, it *literally pays*. As we shared in Chapter 1, our research revealed that effective coaches outperformed their less effective peers by $3.5 million per year. So how do these superstar managers achieve these stellar results? How do they find time to coach amidst the chaos? As we've shared, the most successful sales managers don't coach more. They coach differently. They coach in very targeted ways that lead to better outcomes.

CREATING THE RIGHT
AMOUNT OF STRUCTURE

Good coaching is not some mystical, magical thing that only a few special people are equipped to do. It requires deliberate focus, not Herculean effort. Good coaching requires managers to make better choices during those precious hours they spend coaching their salespeople. It requires managers to fight the tendency of what feels natural or easy and to choose what may feel too structured or restrictive at first. Good coaching is a choice. It is a choice that managers can make to incorporate proven practices that make the desire for effective coaching a day-to-day reality.

Good coaching is not hard, although it does require deliberate intent on the part of the sales manager. There are very specific steps sales managers can take that dramatically improve the quality of their coaching. These steps are not difficult, but they are important. Sales managers who take these steps and practice them consistently outperform managers who don't. They have more satisfied salespeople who perform better. In the balance of this chapter and the ones that follow, we share the steps you can take to dramatically improve the coaching you provide to your sales team.

We liken structured coaching to structured workouts. If you want to get in shape, it is best to develop a workout plan and stick to the plan. You could just go to the gym and meander around, doing a little bit of this and a little bit of that. You would see some incremental improvement, but it's unlikely that you would make great strides in your fitness. On the other hand, if you get together with a personal trainer and map out a workout plan that meets your specific needs, you have a much better chance of becoming fit. There is a much higher likelihood that your workout effort will lead to the desired fitness outcomes.

The same is true with sales coaching. You could do what most sales managers do and have a few coaching discussions here, and a few coaching conversations there. Your coaching efforts could meander in a variety of directions, without real focus, and you would most likely be dissatisfied by the outcome. The outcome most sales managers want from their coaching efforts is to hit their target, meet their quota. Managers who get more of their sellers to quota take a very deliberate approach to coaching. They structure their coaching for maximum impact, the way individuals who are fit structure their workouts. The way successful managers structure their coaching is very straightforward and is described in the sections that follow.

The Importance of Agendas

One of the most important, and often overlooked, elements of effective coaching is the use of an agenda. This seems like an obvious point, but the use of agendas is not as common as you might think. We have a business colleague, Sarah McDonald, whose role includes listening to recorded coaching conversations and evaluating them. She shared that fewer than half of the coaching conversations she has reviewed included a structured agenda. What's fascinating is that these managers recorded their coaching conversations, and they knew they were going to be evaluated. Imagine how this ratio would have changed if no one had been listening.

As you might expect, the coaching sessions with agendas were far more effective than those without. In our own experience with clients, we consistently see a lack of structured agendas when we examine coaching conversations. So, let's agree that agendas are important and useful. They lead to better coaching conversations. A humorous quote by Sarah regarding the use of agendas is this: "Agendas are like Windex. They cure everything."

Establishing a written agenda, agreeing to it at the beginning of the coaching discussion, and then reviewing it at the end of the meeting is a best practice of high-performing sales managers.

> **Agendas are like Windex. They cure everything.**

So, how do you develop an effective agenda for your coaching conversations? Well, we will get into specifics of agenda content in later chapters; however, there are a few best and worst practices to consider. One of the most important aspects of agenda development is the notion that less is better. It is useful to have fewer agenda items and cover those items in more depth. The most common practices—which are *not* best practices—are to either *not* have an agenda or have *too many* agenda items. Either of these extremes will kill the effectiveness of your coaching efforts. Let me provide two real-life examples.

While working with a team of sales managers in one of our client organizations, we were discussing the importance of agendas. One manager, Bill, spoke up and heartily agreed that agendas mattered. He proudly shared that he used very structured agendas when he conducted his one-on-one sessions with his salespeople. He asked if we wanted to see the agenda he used with his team. Well, of course we were curious and wanted to allow Bill to get the recognition he deserved.

We promptly displayed his agenda for all to see. Bill's agenda had 15 items. We asked Bill if these one-on-one sessions were his primary venue for coaching, and he said yes. Most of the coaching he provided to his salespeople occurred during these sessions. We asked Bill if he would mind digging into the agenda items so we could better understand the content of each item. We discussed the content and typical time allotment for each agenda item. At the end of the discussion, we determined that the average one-on-one included about six minutes of coaching. This was a big wake-up call for Bill. He realized that he either needed to eliminate some of the agenda items or allocate significantly more time for his one-on-one sessions to allow for more coaching.

Contrast Bill's experience with that of Mark. Mark was a hotshot seller and was relatively new to sales management. Mark was not a structure sort of guy, and he shared that agendas might be good for other managers, but he didn't need them. Nice idea, not a good fit. Well, it doesn't really help to argue with someone with such a well-entrenched opinion. We find it is always better to allow a bit of self-discovery.

We organized an opportunity for Mark to conduct a coaching conversation with a salesperson with the benefit of a dedicated observer. The observer's job was to capture what happened during the coaching session and provide feedback for Mark. As you might expect, Mark chose to omit the use of an agenda and just allowed the conversation to unfold freely. At the end of the coaching session, we asked Mark whether he thought it was effective. His answer, a resounding yes! He felt it was productive, collaborative, and led to a good outcome.

Well, Mark's perspective changed a bit when the observer provided him with detailed feedback. You see, the observer had an agenda and a checklist of the important things that needed to be covered in the coaching session. The agenda was very targeted and precise. No fluff. The observer proceeded to review each item and the degree to which it was covered effectively. Turns out that Mark missed two very important items. Missed them completely. And here's the most interesting thing: Mark didn't realize he had missed anything. He was shocked. Mark went on to say that not only did he miss important things in the coaching session he had just conducted, but he lamented that he probably missed important things in most of his coaching conversations—and he didn't even know it! Nothing like a little failure to increase our receptivity to change. Mark became a convert, and from that moment forward, he decided to use agendas for his coaching discussions.

Inputs and Meeting Preparation

Just as agendas help ensure that coaching discussions are productive, preparation for the meetings matters as well. The degree to which the manager and the seller come equipped with the right information determines the depth and breadth of the coaching that unfolds. Preparation leads to rich discussions. Lack of preparation leads to superficial discussions. There's just no way around it. You have to put in the time and come ready to actively participate.

The need for preparation is one of the key reason why the most effective coaches conduct fewer coaching conversations with their salespeople compared with lower-performing managers. High-performing managers spend almost as much time *preparing* for coaching as they spend *coaching*. These highly effective coaches also require their salespeople to come equipped and ready to discuss agenda topics. They have very little tolerance for wasting precious one-on-one time grappling for necessary information. As is often the case, a little comparison is in order.

> High-performing sales managers spend almost as much time *preparing* for coaching as they spend coaching.

Let's start with Diego, a very successful sales manager. His commitment to meeting preparation was impressive. For each of his one-on-one coaching sessions, Diego expected each of his salespeople to come prepared to discuss three current opportunities. Diego had criteria for his sellers to use to help them select the three opportunities. Guess what? His sellers were always prepared and had all of the necessary information to have rich discussions about each opportunity.

Diego also required that each salesperson communicate their selected opportunities ahead time so that he could go into the customer relationship management (CRM) system and review the notes. Both manager and salesperson were armed with the information needed to make meaningful progress to move the opportunity forward. It is probably no surprise that Diego's team had significantly higher close rates than the team members of other, less rigorous managers.

Contrast Diego's approach with Tim, another manager in the same company. We observed Tim in action, and it was a rather frustrating experience. Tim was very dissatisfied with his salespeople's lack of diligence using their CRM. It seemed that his salespeople were very slack in their CRM updates, and it was a constant problem when it came time for the forecast. Tim was always chasing his reps down and riding herd on them to update the system. This lack of updating also created wasted time during coaching discussions. We were sympathetic and wanted to help Tim improve his team's CRM usage—as well as improve his overall approach to coaching.

We had the good fortune of being in the room with Tim while he coached one of his salespeople. When we observe a manager in action, we see things that are difficult to uncover during an interview. One of the first things we noticed was that Tim had his computer turned so that both he and his salesperson could see the screen. On the computer screen was his salesperson's instance of the CRM—meaning Tim could do real-time updates to his salesperson's information.

As the coaching conversation unfolded, Tim proceeded to update each opportunity as it was discussed. Tim asked all the questions, most of which were met with "Uh, I'm not sure" or "I'll have to check on that." It is also useful to note that the salesperson had no notes, no computer, not even a notebook. *Nothing at all.* There was absolutely no evidence of seller preparation for the coaching discussion. Tim was doing all the work, all the heavy lifting. Tim had 10 salespeople on his team. No wonder he was stressed. Tim needed to take some of his cues from Diego and require a whole lot more preparation from his salespeople.

Outputs, Accountability, and the Importance of Note-Taking

Whereas preparation leads to richer coaching discussions, accountability leads to better execution of the great ideas shared during those discussions. What do we mean by "accountability"? Well, plainly stated, accountability means the salesperson owns the commitments made during coaching discussions. If the goal of a coaching discussion is to help a salesperson sell more stuff, a series of decisions are likely made, and associated actions must be taken.

Most of the actions are on the part of the salesperson. These decisions and associated actions form the lifeblood of coaching, and when executed properly, they lead to better performance. That is why sales managers coach, to achieve the best possible performance from their salespeople. Accountability is critical, and it all too often falls to the sales manager, not the salesperson. How does this happen?

> Accountability means the salesperson owns the commitments made during the coaching discussion.

We will share another coaching observation to make this point. We were listening remotely to a coaching conversation between a sales manager and one of her team members. Cheryl, the sales manager, had a large team that was geographically dispersed across three states. Because she covered such a wide geography, Cheryl conducted most of her one-on-one coaching discussions by phone. We listened to the hour-long discussion and noted that at least 10 separate commitments had been made regarding actions to be taken by the salesperson she was coaching. A lot of follow-up is required for 10 commitments. This salesperson was going to be busy. Maybe. Or . . . maybe not.

Although Cheryl and her salesperson had a very collaborative and productive discussion, we got a sinking feeling that many of the commitments would not be kept. At the end of the coaching discussion, we had a short debrief with Cheryl. During the debrief, we asked Cheryl how she ensured that her salespeople *did* the things they committed to doing. At first, she was confused by the question. When she realized what we were asking, she got a bit defensive. "Do you mean you expect me to ask my salespeople to take notes and send them to me? Really? That seems pushy. My salespeople are tenured, and it would feel insulting to me to ask them to take notes." We understood her dilemma.

The real problem is that our brains are not wired to keep a lot of information in short-term memory. We have only so much room. When something new comes in, something else goes out. It is not possible to remember the 10 commitments that were made in an hour-long discussion without writing them down. When we explained this to Cheryl, she agreed. Managers *always* take notes during coaching discussions. The problem is that they are taking notes about actions that their *salespeople* must execute. Note-taking is critical. It leads to better follow-through. But follow-through for whom? The manager or the seller? Managers must ensure that their salespeople take detailed notes.

The best way we have found for ensuring that sellers take notes is to require a summary e-mail after the conclusion of each coaching conversation that details agreed-upon actions and commitments. It is impossible for a salesperson to do this without taking notes. This excellent practice has two additional benefits. First, it gives the sales manager a tangible way to hold sellers accountable and check to see if agreed-upon actions have been taken. Second, it removes the dependence on the sales manager to be the note-taker. The accountability lands where it belongs, with the salesperson.

A final note regarding accountability concerns the act of revisiting action items from prior meetings. A critical part of an effective agenda should involve a review of action items, status, and progress from prior meetings. There's no real point in capturing action items if there is no accountability of whether those actions have been taken. Back to our colleague Sarah. In her review of the coaching conversations of 65 managers across six organizations, *not a single manager* reviewed action items from prior coaching conversations. Not one! So, require your salespeople to take notes, have them send you a summary of the agreements via e-mail, and use that e-mail as part of your *agenda* for the following coaching meeting.

CONDUCTING EFFECTIVE COACHING CONVERSATIONS

To this point, we've addressed the importance of preparation and accountability to enable better coaching conversations. We've highlighted the importance of agendas and made the point that fewer items, covered in more depth, lead to better coaching conversations. We've explored how the right type of preparation helps ensure that coaching conversations unfold in ways that create value for both the manager and the salesperson. Preparation, agendas, and accountability are all best practices that set us up for good coaching; however, good coaching happens in *conversations* between the sales manager and the salesperson. It is necessary to dive a bit deeper into the dynamics of the coaching conversation and how to ensure that it unfolds in the most effective way.

One of the interesting things about good coaching conversations is that they are remarkably similar to good sales calls. If you reflect on effective sales calls that you've either conducted or observed, you will begin to see the similarities. For example, good sales calls are highly collaborative. They have a good balance of back-and-forth between the customer and the salesperson. They typically include both seeking and giving on the part of the salesperson. Questions are asked to better understand the customer's environment, and information is typically provided by the seller to address some aspect of customer needs. Good sales calls occur when the seller is prepared, has an agenda, and accomplishes some actionable next step as a result of the sales call.

> Good coaching conversations are remarkably similar to good sales calls. They are highly collaborative, include a good balance of give-and-take, and result in actionable next steps.

Good coaching conversations follow a similar pattern. The coach and the seller are prepared. An agenda is agreed upon. There is a balance of give-and-take on the part of the manager and the seller. They are highly collaborative, incorporate powerful questions, and result in actionable next steps. The attributes we just shared are not reserved for good sales calls and good coaching conversations. They are true for *all* effective conversations. For this reason, we offer a conversation model as opposed to a coaching model. Coaching is just one type of collaborative conversation. The model in Figure 5.1 is one that you can use as a guide to help you conduct effective coaching conversations with your salespeople.

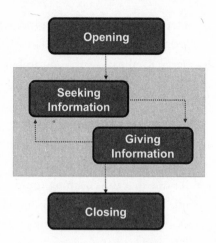

FIGURE 5.1 **Coaching Conversation Model**

Opening

The opening allows the coach to set the stage for an effective coaching conversation. It includes an agenda, agreement on time frame, and desired outcome. The opening lays the groundwork for a productive, collaborative dialogue. Without setting the stage with an effective opening, the coaching discussion can quickly go off the rails.

Many sales managers have told me that they prefer to just let the conversation unfold naturally. They let the salespeople determine what they will discuss. We've observed coaching conversations that unfold this way. They are often a disaster. They are ineffective for the same reason that unstructured sales calls are ineffective. They feel chaotic. Good coaches start their coaching discussion by setting the stage with an effective agenda, and they gain agreement on the desired outcomes. Again, this is remarkably similar to the opening of a good sales call.

> Good coaches open their coaching conversations
> by setting the stage with an effective agenda and
> gaining agreement on desired outcomes.

The opening is a very short, yet extremely important part of the conversation structure. When done well, it creates clarity of intent, establishes parameters and boundaries for the conversation, and increases the chances that the conversation will be productive and valuable for the salesperson. Because the opening is so important to the outcome of the coaching conversation, we will explore an example of how a good opening could unfold. We will systematically unpack an example of a coaching conversation between our sales manager Nick and Megan, one of his salespeople.

It is useful to point out that the coaching topics in our example are not important. We could provide any one of a hundred different topic areas. It doesn't matter for our purposes here. What matters is how Nick navigates the conversation with Megan, not the specific topics he chooses to discuss. We will explore the coaching practices Nick uses throughout the dialogue with the understanding that that the exact topic is largely irrelevant for our purposes. We will explore Nick's approach and determine how his approach affects his coaching effectiveness. We start by examining how Nick opens the conversation.

EXAMPLE

Opening the Coaching Conversation

Nick: Good morning, Megan. Come on in and sit down. How are you today?

Megan: Hi, Nick. I'm fine. I have a few things I need to talk to you about this morning. I'm having an issue with one of my accounts, and I need your help.

Nick: OK, Megan. Certainly. We can discuss your issue once we get through the core of our discussion today. We will leave some time toward the end to address your account issue and any other topics you'd like to discuss.

Megan: Sounds good.

Nick: OK, Megan. We agreed that we are going to discuss three of your stalled opportunities to see if we can figure out how to get them going again. Was that your understanding as well?

Megan: Yes, Nick. That's right.

Nick: Great. Did you come with three specific stalled deals in mind?

Megan: Yes, I did. I'd like to talk about the Sports Den, the National Conference Center, and the Home Away Hotel.

Nick: OK, Megan. Let's start with the Sports Den and then move on to the National Conference Center. Depending on how long each of those take, we may have to move our discussion of the Home Away Hotel for our next one-on-one. I want to ensure that we address your account issue. We have an hour, and as you know, that goes quickly.

Megan: Sounds good.

DEBRIEF

As we mentioned, the opening is typically quick. It is a very small portion of the overall coaching conversation; however, it sets the tone for the rest of discussion. In this example, there were several things Nick did well. First, he created rapport and asked Megan how she was. This may seem trivial, but it isn't. Sellers need to know that their sales managers care about them as people. That although they are preparing to discuss business, they are two people who have lives outside of business. The rapport building could have taken a few more minutes, but it wouldn't have gone on for 15 minutes. A couple of minutes is typically sufficient for the sales manager to connect with the salesperson.

The second thing that Nick did well was clarify the intent of the meeting. He confirmed with Megan that their meeting would include a discussion of three stalled deals. Megan had other things on her mind, which is not uncommon. She raised the need to discuss an account issue. This was clearly something Megan needed to address, and she needed Nick's help. Realistically, Nick couldn't ignore her issue. It had to be addressed; however, it shouldn't hijack their coaching discussion.

Nick very deftly incorporated the additional agenda item, but he moved it toward the end of the meeting. This was very intentional on his part. He was willing to make an adjustment, but he did it in a way that did not impede the treatment of their core agenda topics. He even suggested that they may have to delay their discussion of the third stalled deal so that they could make sure Megan's issue would be addressed. Nick showed Megan that he was listening, cared about addressing her issue, and at the same time, was committed to sticking to the primary intent of their meeting. Nick did an effective job opening the conversation and setting the stage for a productive coaching conversation with Megan.

Now, let's examine what Nick did *not* do. He didn't let Megan's urgent issue hijack the conversation. He handled it, but he did so in a way that maintained the integrity and intent of the coaching discussion. He didn't stick to the exact details of the agenda and discuss all three opportunities. He elected to discuss only two, at an appropriate level of depth, and allow space to discuss Megan's issue. Nick showed flexibility by adjusting the agenda, but he did not lose the intent of the coaching conversation. Nick also chose not to cover Megan's issue *first*. This was a very smart move on his part. Had he added Megan's issue as the first agenda item, it is likely that the discussion would have consumed the bulk of their time together. Discussing the issue toward the end of the meeting ensured that it was addressed in an efficient manner.

Seeking Information

Seeking information is the primary behavior that creates collaboration. It requires preparation and rarely happens naturally. Effective seeking—or questioning—during coaching conversations becomes easier over time with continued practice. The interesting thing about effective coaching questions is that they rarely occur spontaneously. They require thought and planning. Which questions the coach asks the seller are dependent on the topic being discussed. When the coach does not prepare good questions prior to the coaching conversation, the tendency is to give too much information—

to tell the seller what to do. This is the same dynamic that occurs when sellers don't prepare well for sales calls. They talk too much. Same for coaching conversations. Although seeking information and giving information occur in a collaborative, iterative way, seeking must come first. It is for this reason that seeking is prioritized over giving in the conversation model.

In addition to promoting better collaboration, good coaching questions help salespeople develop critical thinking skills. Questions enable the sales manager to understand the seller's perspective. It is far easier to provide helpful coaching if you know where the help is needed. Good questions force sellers to think, to share their point of view, and to problem solve, which are all elements of critical thinking. Critical thinking is a core aspect of agility in salespeople, and it is something that sales managers are in a unique position to bring about through their coaching efforts.

> **Good coaching questions drive collaboration and build the critical thinking skills of your salespeople.**

Let's return to the conversation unfolding between Nick and Megan to get a firsthand look at how good questions enable effective dialog. Nick begins the seeking portion of the discussion by sticking to his agenda and exploring the first stalled account Megan wanted to discuss.

EXAMPLE

Seeking Information

Nick: So, let's start with the Sports Den. That was one of the stalled deals you wanted to discuss. I know this was on your forecast for several months, and you recently took it off. Tell me, what happened that caused this deal to stall?

Megan: Well, it is a real opportunity. The facilities director at the Sports Den has a serious issue with noise in the main floor arena. The coaches have to scream for the players to hear them if a game is going on above them. The facilities director went to the general manager about the issue and got agreement to fund the installation of ceiling panels to reduce the noise. The general manager agreed that it was a big enough issue to fix. That's why I put it on the forecast back in June.

Nick: What's changed? Was the funding pulled, or was there some other issue?

Megan: The general manager got sick and was out for over a month. The facilities director wasn't willing to move forward with the project while the general manager was out. I understood that and didn't pressure him to start the project.

Nick: I can certainly understand the sensitivity of this situation. That was four months ago. I'm guessing the general manager is back at work? Are things back to normal?

Megan: Yes, Nick. He's been back for two months. He seems fine according to the facilities director. I spoke with the director several times in the month the general manager returned to work. They had several discussions about the project and decided to put it on hold for the time being.

Nick: So, what do you think happened? Is the project dead or just delayed?

Megan: Well, the director told me it was just delayed, but now he isn't returning my calls or responding to my e-mails. He's gone dark.

Nick: Yes, I know what that's like. It is very frustrating when you have a deal you think you've won, only to have it go sideways. Let me ask you, Megan, have you ever met with the general manager, or have all of your interactions been with the facilities director?

Megan: I haven't met with the general manager. The facilities director assured me that he was the decision-maker and that the general manager was just the final sign-off and would act on the director's recommendation.

Nick: Well, it seems that the general manager played a more significant role in the decision-making process. What do you think is really happening here? Why do you think the facilities director has gone dark?

Megan: I agree, there's more to the story than the director led me to believe. During several of my discussion with the facilities director, he did mention a possible expansion of the facility. They were considering adding another arena.

DEBRIEF

Although this is only a portion of the coaching conversation between Nick and Megan, it warrants a closer look to see what is happening. In this case, Nick is digging into the details of the opportunity to see how Megan has approached it thus far. He's doing this to better understand the specifics of the opportunity, what it is and why it stalled, so he can determine how best to help. By getting a more thorough understanding of Megan's approach, Nick can isolate trouble spots and provide relevant coaching to help move the opportunity forward.

When seeking information, the use of open- and closed-ended questions and the sequence in which they are used contribute to collaborative dialogue. In addition, the use of empathy is a very powerful interpersonal behavior that helps ensure that the *seeking* portion of the dialogue doesn't feel intrusive. We will highlight how Nick used questions to navigate this portion of the dialogue, as well as the way he incorporated empathetic statements.

In this example, Nick asked quite a few questions before he started honing in on a potential problem area. He asked a combination of open and closed questions to gain information and test Megan's perception of the situation. Open-ended questions are very useful because they tend to elicit a thorough response, contributing to a more collaborative dialogue. Closed-ended questions typically elicit shorter responses, but they are sometimes more realistic in the context of the conversation. Open-ended questions are useful early in the dialogue because they tend to be more general in nature. As additional details are discussed, closed-ended questions may be necessary obtain specific information.

In the above example, Nick started the discussion of the Sports Den by asking Megan, *"Tell me, what happened that caused the deal to stall?"* Nick was casting a wide net with this general and open-ended question, and it elicited a substantial response from Megan. However, Megan's immediate answer didn't give Nick any information about why the deal was stalled. Nick had to ask several additional questions before he got any really useful information.

A bit later in the dialogue, Nick switched gears. Nick asked Megan, *"Have you ever met with the general manager, or have all of your interactions been with the facilities director?"* This was a closed-ended question. It was the right question to ask. The question could have felt awkward and potentially forced had Nick attempted to make this question open-ended. It would have sounded unnatural. Nick needed a very specific piece of information, and the closed-ended question worked. He went from broad, open-ended questions to specific, closed-ended questions when needed to get to the right level of detail to inform his coaching efforts. This balance between open and closed, general and specific, questions is natural, realistic, and effective in coaching conversations.

One final best practice Nick displayed in this example was the use of empathy. People want to feel understood. Using empathy tends to put people at ease and makes them feel more comfortable with you as their coach. The use of empathy causes sellers to feel that we, as coaches, are on their side. That we are a team, working on this together. The first example of empathy was when Nick said, *"I can certainly understand the sensitivity of this situation."* He was validating Megan's choice to back off and not pester the facilities director while the general manager was ill.

Another example of empathy was when Nick said, *"Yes, I know what that's like. It is very frustrating when you have a deal you think you've won, only to have it go sideways."* This use of empathy was especially powerful. In the first statement, Nick showed Megan that he has been in this situation himself. The next statement acknowledged Megan's frustration at having a viable deal unravel. Without empathy, sellers may feel defensive and be hesitant to share specific details. Empathy is a very powerful coaching behavior, and it helps create a welcoming environment, one in which sellers feel free to be open and share real information.

Now, let's explore what Nick did *not* do. Nick did not tell Megan that it was a mistake to limit her contact to the facilities director. This may have seemed like an obvious miss on her part. It would have been very tempting for Nick to just tell Megan this was a mistake; but it was much more effective for Nick to get Megan to come to this realization on her own. Nick asked Megan whether she had met with the general manager. This question was necessary to inspect Megan's actions— to find out what really happened. Inspection can feel uncomfortable; however, it is necessary to help determine what kind of coaching is needed. Inspection, when used appropriately, is a powerful pivot point that paves the way for good coaching.

One final note about seeking information. We hearken back to our colleague Sarah McDonald and her detailed analysis of recorded coaching conversations. Sarah found that 70 percent of managers had room for improvement in their ability to engage the salesperson during the coaching conversation. This lack of engagement does not bode well for the effectiveness of most coaching conversations in her analysis, and it likely does not bode well for most coaching conversations unfolding regularly between sales managers and salespeople. In addition to a dearth of seeking behaviors, most managers in her analysis also failed gain salesperson feedback on the effectiveness of the coaching they provided. A few final questions to consider are, "What was most valuable or helpful about this conversation? What could have been improved?" Questions like these cause salespeople to feel valued, and they help sales managers continuously improve.

Giving Information

Giving information, in the form of direction or guidance, is an important element of the conversation model. Sales managers are typically very comfortable providing direction and guidance during coaching, just as salespeople are very comfortable providing information during a sales call. The issue occurs when either *too much* information is shared or the information that is shared is *not relevant*. Good coaching questions help the sales manager determine which information needs to be shared. Good coaches, like good salespeople, ensure that the information they provide is relevant and valuable to the conversation.

> Good coaches, like good salespeople, ensure that the information they provide is relevant and valuable to the conversation.

The balance of giving and seeking will depend highly on the salesperson being coached. More tenured or highly skilled salespeople often require less guidance than their less experienced peers. It can be awkward and uncomfortable to use a highly seeking approach when coaching an inexperienced seller. These less skilled sellers often don't know what to do in any given situation, and they require more direction than their more experienced peers. It is important for sales managers to adjust the level of collaboration depending on the skills and experience of the salesperson being coached. Collaboration is always helpful. It is the balance of giving and seeking that must be adjusted.

We return to the conversation unfolding between Nick and Megan to examine how Nick uses the information he has obtained thus far through his questioning efforts. In this next example, Nick provides direction to Megan, but he does so in a way that encourages collaboration.

A Blend of Seeking and Giving Information

Nick: Megan, from what you've told me so far, it appears that there are two possible reasons why the deal stalled. First, the general manager may have been more instrumental in the decision than you originally thought he was. And, second, you mentioned another project under consideration.

Let's talk a bit more about the general manager for a moment. What do you know about this person? Why do you think he was willing to fund the project initially?

Megan: I met him at one of the Sports Den's open houses. I only spoke with him briefly. I think he agreed to fund the project because of the noise complaints from the coaches. When the facilities director approached him about the funding, I believe it was on the heels of several complaints about the noise in that particular arena. You know, the squeaky wheel getting the grease. Coaches were complaining.

Nick: I see. So, it seems that he was well aware of the problem, not just acting on a recommendation from the facilities director.

Megan: Yes, I believe so.

Nick: Did you ask to have a joint meeting with both the facilities director and the general manager?

Megan: No, I didn't. I really didn't think it was necessary.

Nick: If you had asked, do you think the facilities director would have complied and arranged the meeting?

Megan: I'm not sure. Maybe.

Nick: How do you think this situation would be different if the general manager had been more involved? If you had been able to explore just how big the noise problem was—from his perspective?

Megan: Well, it might have expedited things. I might have been able to get a contract signed before he went out on leave.

Nick: Yes, I agree. It is looking like the general manager was the cause of the delay. At what point in your conversations with the facilities

director would it have been most helpful to get the general manager involved?

Megan: When he was going for funding approval. If I could have helped
the facilities director make the case and help the general manager
see how quickly we could eliminate the noise problem and reduce
the complaints, I think this project would already be under way.

Nick: It is certainly possible. I think it is always a good idea to get to the
highest level of decision-maker possible in order to get the deal. If
the general manager was truly the ultimate decision-maker, and it
seems likely he was in this case, it could only have helped.

Let's talk about the expansion project—to build another arena.
You said the facilities director mentioned that in some of your conversations. Do you know whether that project was funded?

Megan: I think so, but I'm not sure.

Nick: It's possible that it came down to a choice of which project to
fund—fix the noise problem or build a new arena. I guess you won't
know until you speak to the facilities director. What do you think
about stopping by the Sports Den to see if construction has begun? Maybe you would run into the facilities director and have a
chance to reignite the conversation. What do you think about that
idea?

Megan: I could certainly stop by. I have nothing to lose at this point.

DEBRIEF

In this portion of the dialogue, we examine the interplay between seeking and giving behaviors. We highlight the techniques Nick used to
help Megan understand some of the possible flaws in her approach,
as well as specific things she could have done differently when pursuing this deal.

The first coaching practice we'd like to highlight is the use of *summarizing*. Nick summarized what he'd heard Megan say about two possible issues with the deal. Nick said, "*Megan, from what you've told*

me so far, it appears that there are two possible reasons why the deal stalled. First, the general manager may have been more instrumental in the decision than you originally thought he was. And, second, you mentioned another project under consideration." This showed active listening on Nick's part, and it had the added benefit of keeping the conversation focused on targeted areas for coaching.

Summarizing key points keeps the conversation focused and shows the salesperson that you are actively listening.

Nick followed up his summary with a good, open-ended question about the general manager. He asked, *"What do you know about this person? Why do you think he was willing to fund the project initially?"* This forced Megan to think, to provide meaningful commentary about her experience. Nick then followed up with three pointed closed-ended questions. He asked, *"So, he was well aware of the problem, not just acting on a recommendation from the facilities director?"* and *"Did you ask to have a joint meeting with both the facilities director and the general manager?"* and *"If you had asked, do you think the facilities director would have complied and arranged the meeting?"* All three of these questions were designed to make Megan aware that she should have gotten a meeting with the general manager and didn't. Having Megan say it herself, acknowledge it, was much more powerful than having Nick tell her she should have met with the general manager.

So, this portion of the dialog was probably a bit uncomfortable for Megan; however, it was a very powerful way for Nick to get his point across and create awareness for Megan. Nick then shifted back to an open question that got Megan to reflect on how this could have been different. He asked, *"How do you think this situation would be different if the general manager had been more involved? If you had been able to explore just how big the noise problem was—from his perspective?"* This open-ended question got Megan to articulate how the deal progression could have changed if she had been at the right level of contact. Again, it is not about the specifics of this scenario as much as it is about best practices. By using a good open-ended question at this point in the conversation, Nick forced Megan to think about how her deal could have unfolded differently. He forced her to consider how alternative action on her part could have changed the trajectory of the outcome. In other words, Nick forced Megan to engage in critical thinking.

As a follow-up to his series of questions to Megan, Nick made a statement that reinforced his perspective concerning an alternative approach. He said, *"I think it is always a good idea to get to the highest level of decision-maker possible in order to get the deal. If the general manager was truly the ultimate decision-maker, and it seems likely he was in this case, it could only have helped."* Nick was giving information—in this case, affirmation that it could have been useful to get to a higher level of decision-maker. Making statements to reinforce critical learning points helps increase the likelihood that sellers will behave differently in the future.

The final practice we'd like to highlight in this dialogue was when Nick made a recommendation in the form of a question. He asked, *"What do you think about stopping by the Sports Den to see if construction has begun? Maybe you would run into the facilities director and have a chance to reignite the conversation. What do you think about that idea?"* This is important to highlight because it was very subtle and could easily be overlooked. Nick could have told Megan to stop by the Sports Den and check out the construction status, as well as do her best to run into the facilities director while she was there. He did not.

The best sales coaches make recommendations
in the form of questions. This gives the
salesperson the opportunity to own the idea.

Nick made a suggestion in the form of a question, and then asked Megan for her reaction. This subtle difference, between providing direction versus suggesting a possible direction, have very different implications. When Nick suggested a potential course of action and asked for Megan's reaction, he was allowing her to take ownership of the idea. Nick allowed Megan to feel empowered during the conversation, to choose whether to take a certain course of action. Psychologically speaking, we all like our own ideas best. As a coach, you can dramatically increase the likelihood of appropriate action if you get your sellers more actively involved in the development of the idea.

Nick did *not* fall into the trap of telling Megan what she did wrong. This is an extremely common (and deceptively efficient) way to coach. It is the *lazy* way to coach. It requires less effort, but it has less impact. Nick did *not* tell Megan that she should have met with the general manager. He also avoided telling her how this opportunity could have unfolded differently if she had. He did not take the easy way out. Nick helped build Megan's critical thinking skills.

Closing

Finally, effective coaching discussions end with actionable next steps. Decisions are made throughout the course of the coaching conversation, and commitments are made. A review of these decisions and agreed-upon actions is the best way to close the conversation. As mentioned earlier, it is much more effective if the salesperson is the one summarizing the discussion and reviewing the agreed-upon next steps.

> Having the salesperson summarize the decisions and the agreed-upon actions is a best practice.

Let's see how Nick and Megan wrapped up their coaching conversation. We are fast-forwarding to the end of their conversation for purposes of illustration. In this next portion of the transcript, we see how the conversation was concluded and how Nick's behavior helped to ensure effective action for Megan.

EXAMPLE

Closing the Coaching Conversation

Nick: Well, Megan, we've discussed two of your stalled opportunities, as well as a solution to the service issue you brought forth. Can you please review your understanding of any major lessons learned, agreements we made, and actionable next steps for each of these topics—to make sure we are on the same page?

Megan: Sure, Nick. Let's start with the Sports Den. My next step is to drop by and see if any construction is under way regarding the new arena. I hope to see the facilities director while I'm there and reignite our opportunity. It became pretty clear that it would have been very helpful to speak with the general manager while I was pursuing the opportunity. It might have solidified the deal.

Nick: Yes, Megan. It is quite possible that the Sports Den opportunity could have turned out differently with the involvement of the general manager. I look forward to learning what you find when you stop by. Now how about the National Conference Center?

Megan: We agreed that I should set up a referral call between the logistics manager and one of our other conference center clients. The logistics manager is worried about unforeseen issues getting in the way of a successful project. We agreed that a reference call with a successful project in the same industry would be helpful in reducing the logistic manager's feeling of risk. This is probably a good idea for all opportunities where the decision-maker is worried about moving forward.

Nick: Yep, on track so far. How about the service issue?

Megan: Well, we agreed to have our quality manager contact this client to better understand the noise issue and see if everything was installed correctly. That will be our initial step. Once we get that information, we can determine the best path forward.

Nick: OK, Megan, I think that about covers it. Thanks for your time and your preparation. I feel like we made good progress today. How about you?

Megan: Me too, Nick. This was extremely helpful, particularly the discussion of my stalled deals.

Nick: All right, Megan. As usual, please send me a quick follow-up e-mail summarizing our commitments. We can revisit them as needed to make sure we stay on track.

Megan: Sure, Nick. Will do.

DEBRIEF

As with the opening of the conversation, the closing will most likely be brief. The meat of the coaching conversation happens with the seeking and giving components. The close is designed to ensure that commitments are kept and follow-up happens. It is an opportunity to ensure that key coaching points were heard and internalized.

The first thing Nick did well in the close of the discussion was to quickly recap the major topics that were discussed. This acted as a primer for Megan to ensure that her summary was comprehensive and included all three topics. Next, Nick was very clear about the kind of information he expected Megan to include in her summary. Nick specifically asked Megan to cover lessons she learned during the discussion, agreements made, and actionable next steps. Nick was very clear in his request, resulting in a thorough summary by Megan. As Megan summarized each point, Nick prompted her to continue to the next topic. In reality, this prompting may not be necessary depending on how thoroughly the salesperson reviews the information. If key points are missed, additional prompting may be required.

Nick also asked Megan about her perception of their progress. This is a quick and easy way to determine whether Megan felt the conversation was valuable. Finally, Nick asked Megan to send a follow-up e-mail detailing their agreements. It is virtually impossible for a salesperson to either summarize commitments at the end of the discussion or summarize in a follow-up e-mail without taking detailed notes. I cannot overemphasize the importance of having the salesperson take notes. Although sales managers always take notes, they are not the ones responsible for taking action. Note-taking increases accountability for action and captures information needed to update the opportunity records within the CRM. This is a common practice of highly successful sales managers.

Asking the salesperson for feedback on the effectiveness of the coaching conversation is a best practice.

What Nick *didn't* do was assume the accountability for reviewing the outcomes of the coaching discussion. Nick could easily have summarized their discussion of each topic. He could have detailed next steps and reinforced lessons learned. In fact, if Nick had done the summary, it would have been more *efficient*. It would have been the quick and easy way to handle this moment. And it would have been less effective. Nick didn't take the easy way out. He took steps to ensure that Megan learned from their discussion and was prepared to take action as a result. He held Megan accountable.

COACHING DOESN'T HAVE
TO BE COMPLICATED

For anyone who's been through coaching training, our model will seem very simple. Simple is good. We've whittled coaching down to its essence. We've done this to make coaching practical, doable, and dare we say, *easy*. We've provided a digestible model to follow that will lead to effective coaching conversations. We've provided practical guidelines for structuring coaching so that it is organized and relevant and has a high impact. Most coaching models are not as user-friendly.

In our work with clients, we always review any prior training they've provided to their sales managers. We encounter many coaching models in this process. In one such case, we were working with the director of learning and development of a large insurance company. The director had trained the company's sales managers using a behavioral coaching program offered by a well-known sales training company. We asked what seemed like obvious questions: If they've already put their sales managers through a coaching program, why did they need another one? What was wrong with the training they'd already provided? Her answer was illuminating, but not surprising.

The director had selected her prior coaching program because the sales training company she was working with was very well known and well respected. The sales training the company deployed had been effective, so by association, she figured the coaching training would be equally effective. But that's not what happened. The director said that the sales managers enjoyed the training and gave it high marks, but there was no evidence that the coaching model was being used. Adoption was nonexistent. Why? Because it was too complex.

She showed me a job aid that was deployed in the training, outlining the model. This behavioral coaching model was thorough—excruciatingly thorough. It involved 12 separate steps. Each of the 12 steps included several substeps. It was very procedural and complicated. We quickly understood why it wasn't being used. The director said, "What sales manager is realistically going to use a 12-step coaching model?" We agreed. Who *would* use such a complicated model? Apparently not *her* sales managers. Probably not *any* sales managers. Surely, not anyone reading this book.

We are very passionate about simplifying sales coaching. Our coaching conversation model is concise, yet comprehensive. Only four steps are needed to have an effective coaching conversation. Sales managers should open the conversation in a way that sets the tone for a productive dialogue, use a balance of seeking and giving information to create the desired level of collaboration, and close the conversation in a way that holds the salesperson accountable. It is easy to develop complex models. It takes a lot more thought to develop something simple, like the conversation model we've put forth. Why such a simple model? Simple models work. Complex models don't.

KEY TAKEAWAYS: STRUCTURING COACHING CONVERSATIONS

- Identifying inputs to coaching conversations ensures that both the salesperson and sales manager are prepared for the discussion. Having relevant information enables more productive coaching discussions and reduces wasted time.

- Agendas keep the conversations on track and ensure that the coaching achieves the desired level of depth. High-performing managers have fewer items and cover those items in greater depth than low-performing managers.

- Capturing agreed-upon action items and having salespeople review and document them is a best practice. This ensures that meeting outputs are more likely to be acted on. It also gives the sales manager vital information that can be reviewed for progress in future coaching meetings.

- Good coaching conversations have predictable structure. They start with an opening that sets the stage for a productive dialogue. They have a balance of giving and seeking to ensure collaboration, and they close with actionable next steps. Good coaching questions improve salespeople's critical thinking skills.

- Asking the salesperson for feedback on coaching effectiveness is a best practice. By asking for feedback, managers can learn tangible ways to adjust coaching their effort to improve overall coaching effectiveness.

- Coaching doesn't have to be complicated. In fact, if it is, managers won't do it. All it takes is four steps to have a rich coaching discussion.

CHAPTER 6

FORMALIZING SALES COACHING INTO YOUR DAY-TO-DAY JOB

On the path to developing effective coaching practices, selecting the right activities to coach is an important first step. Structuring conversations in ways that create value for the salespeople being coached is another important consideration. In addition to knowing *what* you should be coaching, and *how* those conversations can unfold, the way you operationalize coaching interactions into your day-to-day work flow is vital. In fact, this is where most sales managers hit the wall.

There is no point in prioritizing and structuring coaching conversations if you can't figure out how to consistently *conduct* those conversations. It is like developing an intensive exercise plan that isn't realistically going to fit into your real life. You might have a great plan, but that plan is not likely to translate to a fit body. For a coaching plan to be viable, it must be realistic and fit into the job you have.

There are plenty of hard-working sales managers who are failing miserably, and they are looking for a lifeline. Sales managers need a strategy for getting better without having to work harder. They can't expend enough effort to overcome the devastating impacts of poor decisions about what, how, and *when* to coach. The better the coaching decisions, the higher the impact of effort expended. For sales managers who are overworked, under-developed, and mostly underpaid, this is good news indeed.

> Sales managers can't expend enough effort to overcome the devastating impacts of poor decisions about *what, how,* and *when* to coach.

In this chapter, we explore the most common mistakes managers make when attempting to *implement* effective coaching practices. Thankfully, many of the pitfalls managers stumble into that impede their ability to op-erationalize coaching practices are predictable, and avoidable. By examining coaching practices that are common, yet ineffective, we can help managers avoid these pitfalls and get on a path to effective and *consistent* coaching.

In the sections that follow, we explore how formality and coaching frequency affect a manager's ability to turn coaching intentions into coaching practices. We offer research-based guidance on ways to formalize your coaching efforts in ways that are realistic versus idealistic. We provide specific guidance that has been proven to result in more effective coaching and more salespeople at quota.

HOW FORMALITY AFFECTS COACHING

The best way to illustrate the impact of formality is to see how it plays out with real sales managers. We begin the examination of coaching practices with a story of two managers we encountered in one of our client organizations. On the surface, both managers were successful. They worked for the same Fortune 50 company and were both meeting their revenue targets. It was tempting to assume that they were both effective coaches, but that was not the case. Their approach to coaching was remarkably different. Which one was a more effective coach, and why? Read on. You decide.

Ed: A Mover and a Shaker

By all accounts Ed was a rock star. He was far above plan every year. Ed managed a team of four salespeople. The culture within Ed's global Fortune 50 organization demanded that Ed be heralded as *best practice* due to his performance level. We were eager to spend time with Ed and learn what he was doing that was leading to his consistently high revenue attainment.

My colleague and I flew to the hinterlands of Canada to observe him in action. When we called Ed ahead of time to arrange the observation, he seemed a bit perplexed. We told him that we would like to observe a few typical coaching interactions between him and his team members. He seemed a bit bewildered and told us he thought our request was strange. Off to a bad start.

Ed wanted to know what we meant by *coaching interactions*. We told Ed that we wanted to observe him in action, perhaps helping his salespeople strategize opportunities or plan for key sales calls. We suggested that perhaps he could allow us to observe a typical one-on-one coaching session.

"Well, I don't have any formal one-on-ones," Ed told us. "I talk to my sellers all the time, multiple times per day. You want to listen to me talking to my reps?" Ed asked, incredulously. "And you're going to fly all the way out here to do that?"

"Yes," we replied and we picked a date to do just that.

We met him in his office. He invited us to sit down. We began by reviewing his agenda for his time with us. We asked him which meetings he had set up with his sellers, who they were, and what he planned to discuss. He laughed and said, "Oh, I just planned on calling a few people and getting them on the phone. You can listen to our conversations." He did that, and for the next 45 minutes, we heard Ed chatting aimlessly with two salespeople about a variety of topics, some of which involved existing sales cycles.

We learned that Ed didn't have any type of regularly scheduled coaching discussions with his salespeople. At first, we thought he was exaggerating. He wasn't. The only time any planning or coaching took place happened when Ed was attending sales calls. Most conversations Ed had with his salespeople were on an ad hoc or as-needed basis. Ed's interactions with his team members were sporadic and unpredictable.

I must say, Ed was funny. His relationship with his team members was good. He was their *go-to guy*. He was a master salesman, and he told us he was heavily involved in every sale his team made. No sale happened without his involvement, ever! We believed him.

Jack: The Solid Dude

Jack managed a team of 12 salespeople across two different provinces of Canada. When we called Jack to set up a time to conduct our observation, he asked us which type of interactions we would like to see. He said it would probably be best to sit in on a few of his one-on-one sessions with his salespeople, or if we would prefer, we could listen in to his team conference call. We chose to listen in on a few of his one-on-ones. Off to a good start.

When we arrived at Jack's office, he welcomed us and brought us into the conference room where one of his salespeople was already seated and ready for the meeting. The one-on-one began to unfold, starting with an agreement on the agenda. The meeting lasted an hour and covered a discussion of three existing opportunities. Jack and his salesperson discussed opportunity progress, including potential barriers, and agreed-upon next steps. They summarized their meeting, covering time frames and ownership of key tasks. We observed two such meetings—which were remarkably similar in structure, yet different in dialogue. We spent a bit of time debriefing with Jack and learned that these interactions were typical.

What's the Difference?

Jack was not the most charismatic guy. He probably was not the life of the party the way Ed was. However, Jack was clearly in charge of his approach to his team. Not in a controlling way but in an intentional way. It was obvious that his salespeople were prepared for their coaching discussions. It was obvious that Jack was also prepared. Jack had created a coaching formality for himself and his team that reflected the priorities he chose. He was living his sales manager role the way *he* thought he should, and it was working. Jack was calm and matter of fact.

Contrast this with Ed. Ed was very excited and excitable. He was a mover and a shaker. He was a man of action. He was either on the phone with one of his salespeople or out in the field on a sales call. He was a firestorm of activity. He was never bored. He was doing what he wanted to do, when he wanted to do it. Not much formality but lots of action.

You are probably wondering what the real lesson is to this story of Ed and Jack. The contrast is so stark that the insights seem to jump off the page and scream, structure, structure, structure! Not so fast. The obvious insights are rarely useful. It is in the nuances where the gold is mined. Let's take a closer look at the situation with Ed and Jack and identify the story behind the story of Jack's effectiveness.

AD HOC VERSUS FORMAL COACHING

Ed was a whirling dervish of sales activity, and every day was a new adventure. Almost all of Ed's interactions with his salespeople were *ad hoc*. Spontaneous. Just in time. That was why Ed had such difficulty processing our request to observe one of his typical coaching interactions. There were no *typical* coaching interactions. Manage four salespeople this way and you can continue to fly under the radar for a time. Try this approach when managing a larger team and you die!

Contrast Ed's ad hoc approach with Jack's scheduled one-on-one coaching sessions. Jack conducted each interaction in a very similar way.

He and the salesperson were well prepared, and they had a structured agenda. Jack conducted his coaching sessions with incredible consistency. The frequency and content of his coaching were remarkably predictable. They were *formal*. Jack managed a team of 12 salespeople. Jack didn't have the luxury of informality. What Jack needed, and displayed, was the ability to prioritize and *formalize* his coaching effort.

What we didn't tell you was that Ed and Jack were both identified as observation candidates by the vice president of sales. The only problem was that the vice president didn't really like Ed, not that much anyway. Yes, his performance was acknowledged; however, when we interviewed Ed's leadership team, they were very hesitant to say positive things about Ed and rarely wanted him to participate in leadership meetings. The fact that Ed was geographically separated from most of the other leaders gave them an easy out.

We found this ambivalence somewhat confusing and became committed to figuring out what going on with Ed. When we asked what the problem was, the answer was vague—something about Ed's not being a team player and being a bit rogue. When we asked the vice president what "rogue" meant, he just said that Ed did his own thing. He couldn't pinpoint what was wrong. He just knew it was an issue. Hmmm. Not helpful.

What the vice president of sales knew was that he wanted more managers like Jack and fewer like Ed. We solved the mystery of the sales leaders' ambivalence toward Ed and affinity for Jack because we were able to observe them both in action. Ed did everything in an ad hoc manner. His management approach was not predictable or organized in any meaningful way. Ed's coaching was ad hoc, and Jack's coaching was formal. Ed did some things in a formal way, but coaching was not one of them. Jack did some things in an ad hoc manner, but coaching was not one of them.

Coaching Formality Continuum

It is useful to think of sales coaching on a continuum of formality. Figure 6.1 shows that on the low end of the continuum, we have ad hoc and unplanned interactions. On the high end of formality, we have scheduled and repeated interactions. All coaching interactions fall somewhere on the continuum.

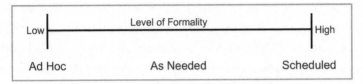

FIGURE 6.1 **Coaching Formality Continuum**

If we contrast Ed and Jack on this continuum, Ed would be toward the low end, and Jack would be toward the high end. Formality is never an all-or-nothing proposition because different types of coaching interactions warrant different levels of formality. We will address the specific types of coaching interactions and the associated formality in the chapters that follow. For now, we examine the nature of interactions across the spectrum and what the research reveals about their effectiveness.

Ad Hoc Coaching Interactions

Ad hoc interactions are unplanned, spontaneous conversations. Examining the nature of ad hoc interactions helps us gain a better understanding of why they are often ineffective. Ad hoc interactions are very prevalent between sales managers and salespeople because they don't require much planning or forethought. This lack of planning and forethought has ramifications. By examining these ramifications, we can be more mindful of the choices we make when coaching our sellers.

Salespeople know how to get what they want. They approach their manager when he's busy. Busy people don't like to get interrupted, and they are likely to do everything they can to get back to what they were doing beforehand. Salespeople are not the only ones who use this sneaky trick. Those of you with children are very familiar with this tactic. The best time for children to ask their parents for something—like money or whether they can have a sleepover with a friend—is when their parents are on the way out the door. In other words, when the parents are *pressed for time*. The parents are just looking to get out the door.

When we are interrupted, our primary goal is to quickly get back to what we were doing before the interruption. We don't collaborate in these situations. We don't probe deeply in these situations. In other words, we don't *coach* in these situations. Ad hoc conversations feel efficient, but they are just not effective. Let's go back to our sales manager Nick and examine an ad hoc conversation he has with one of his salespeople to illustrate this point. In this case, Megan interrupted Nick while he was busy preparing his forecast.

> When we are interrupted, our primary goal is to quickly get back to what we were doing before the interruption.

EXAMPLE

Ad Hoc Conversation

Megan: Hi, Nick, can I talk to you for a minute?

Nick (inward groan, outward smile): Sure, Megan. Come on in.

Megan: Thanks, Nick. I only need a minute. I've got a call with ABC Company later today, and I want to make sure I have my facts straight. When you and I chatted about targeting Relianz customers, ABC is a current Relianz user, and I'd like to begin to explore some upsides for having them switch to our solutions. I was thinking that maybe a special discount for competitive switching could incent them to move our way. What do you think?

Nick: Well, Megan, I haven't really given this much thought. And I was in the middle of putting together my forecast for Anna. What did you have in mind?

Megan: I was thinking maybe a 10 percent discount on the products and perhaps a free assessment of their current soundproofing needs might generate some interest.

Nick: Well, I guess that's not such a big discount. I'm not as sure about the free assessment. That might consume a lot of our sales engineer's time.

Megan: Yeah, I thought about that, Nick, but I think it will go a long way to getting these Relianz users to consider switching.

Nick (looking at his watch): OK, Megan. I guess that makes sense for now. Please let me know how the call goes and whether ABC Company is motivated by the free assessment.

Megan: Thanks, Nick. Will do!

DEBRIEF

On the surface, this seems like a rather mundane interaction; however, when we dig a bit deeper, it becomes more problematic. First, how focused was Nick on Megan and her questions? Not very. Why? Because Nick was in the middle of doing an important and time-bound task. The forecast was due to his boss within the hour. Nick felt compelled to help Megan, so he put his task aside for a moment. Megan got right to the point—which was good—regarding a few strategies she could use to create interest with a potential prospect. She had a few ideas, which was also positive. However, Nick's mind was still on the forecast. In this situation, Nick's primary concern was not to probe deeply into Megan's reasoning but to satisfy her enough to get her out of his office. He needed to finish the forecast.

This is the harsh reality of many ad hoc conversations. Sales managers are not at their best when they are interrupted. None of us are. When we are taken off task, our attention is divided. Managers with divided attention don't tend to provide good coaching. Not because they don't know how to coach, but because the interruption creates an environment that is somewhat *hostile* to coaching.

If Nick had been in a planned coaching discussion with Megan, it is likely that he would have challenged her use of discounting as the best way to generate interest. He could have strategized with her on specific problems her solution could address when compared to the competitive solution. He may have asked Megan a few more questions about her upcoming sales call, such as whom she was meeting with and any prior conversations she'd had. He may have asked her what she knew about the solution already in place. The point is that Nick would have done many things differently had he been in a situation more conducive to sales coaching.

Typical Drivers of Ad Hoc Interactions
- A customer service issue has surfaced and must be addressed immediately.
- A deal that is very close to closing requires an adjustment to contract terms.
- A contract for an existing deal is in legal, and a stipulation must be made.

What all of the above examples have in common is that they are urgent. Urgent events often need immediate attention. This need for attention comes at inopportune times and disrupts other work. It is for this reason that these discussions are rushed, directive, and concise. The types of interactions mentioned above are not necessarily *coaching* interactions. When conversations are ad hoc, they unfold in similar ways, none of which contribute to rich coaching.

The trouble arises when a sales manager falls into the habit of reacting to his salespeople (the way Ed works) instead of proactively scheduling coaching discussions (the way Jack works). When sales managers are primarily reacting to seller requests, they fall into a pattern of engaging in ad hoc conversations for both coaching and noncoaching topics. This is unfortunate because most true coaching discussions can be scheduled.

An overreliance on ad hoc interactions as the primary means of coaching is a direct contributor to the significant disconnect between seller and manager perception of coaching. When managers rely on ad hoc coaching as their go-to approach, the quantity of coaching that managers believe they are providing is vastly different than the quantity of coaching sellers believe they are receiving. Managers who incorporate even a minimum level of formality into their coaching dramatically improve the quality, and perceived quantity, of their sales coaching.

Managers who incorporate even a minimal amount of formality into their coaching dramatically improve the quality, and perceived quantity, of their sales coaching.

As-Needed Coaching Interactions

Some coaching interactions cannot be conducted *far in advance*, but they can be *planned*. As-needed coaching interactions are typically scheduled, one-time events related to a near-term sales activity. Sales managers must maintain flexibility to provide coaching as needed to address business demands.

A deal may have changed course and need near-term attention. A salesperson may have secured a meeting with an important contact in an existing opportunity and could benefit from a planning discussion. A salesperson may have been notified of his or her inclusion in a finalist presentation. These scenarios have one thing in common: they are not regularly occurring events. They are time bound, somewhat urgent, and need coaching attention.

Typical Drivers of As-Needed, Planned Interactions

- A proposal is due, and the team must collaborate on the content.

- An important sales call is coming up and must be planned.

- A deal has been lost, and a post mortem must be conducted.

Because these situations are not regularly occurring, they cannot be scheduled in a formal, repeatable way; however, they are very important.

These types of as-needed discussions occur throughout a manager's week and cannot be easily anticipated. The more important the activity, the more critical for the manager and the salesperson to schedule time to discuss it.

Planned coaching discussions tend to be more focused, more robust, and overall more effective than ad hoc interactions. The manager and salesperson can set an appropriate amount of time for the discussion, agree on an agenda and desired outcomes, and come to the meeting prepared. All of these structuring elements lead to better coaching interactions. While it is tempting to conduct coaching discussions as events arise, it is almost always better to plan a time for the discussion—even if the scheduled time is within the same day.

> Planned coaching interactions are more focused, robust, and effective than ad hoc interactions.

Scheduled Coaching Interactions

Some coaching topics lend themselves to regularly scheduled interactions. Discussions of the pipeline, strategizing complex deals, and strategizing an approach to key accounts are all topics that benefit from regularly scheduled, *recurring* coaching interactions. Depending upon the nature of the salesperson's role, some combination of these topics is always relevant. These types of topics unfold over time, and the specifics of each *change* over time. In other words, these topics require consistent, focused attention and coaching.

Typical Scheduled Recurring Coaching Interactions

- Pipeline reviews

- Territory reviews

- Account plans and reviews

These three topics are recurring, strategically important, and have some type of regularity to them. You may have noticed that I mentioned coaching *topics*, not types of coaching meetings. These topics may be discussed in one-on-one meetings, account team meetings, a mixture of salespeople and specialists, or even within the management team. We will address the nature of meeting topics, typical frequencies, and most common formats in later chapters.

What the Research Says

So, what are the big takeaways regarding which level of coaching formality is most effective? Formality is tricky because it is not equally effective in all situations. The type of coaching topic tends to drive the level of formality required. Topics that are very time sensitive in nature tend to benefit from as-needed coaching discussions. Topics that are more predictable and longer term tend to benefit from scheduled, recurring interactions.

We acknowledge that ad hoc conversations happen and that they're often necessary, but they are not the best format for coaching. It is difficult, if not impossible, to effectively measure ad hoc coaching conversations without a time study. In lieu of a time study, we have some overarching findings that support higher versus lower levels of coaching formality.

High-performing managers are more likely to exhibit the following patterns of coaching as compared to their lower-performing peers:

- They schedule coaching conversations.

- They keep their scheduled coaching sessions a higher percentage of the time.

- They conduct coaching conversations less frequently.

- They conduct longer, more in-depth discussions.

In the chapters that follow, we will provide specific findings regarding which types of conversations benefit most from a more formal coaching approach and which ones lend themselves to as-needed coaching.

For now, we are going to examine the nature of formality and the common traps sales managers encounter when they attempt to formalize their coaching approach.

> High-performing sales managers conduct scheduled coaching conversations less frequently and for longer durations than their lower-performing peers.

FORMALITY AS A MECHANISM FOR INSPECTION

Not all scheduled, recurring interactions are *coaching* interactions. *Coaching* involves helping a salesperson do something better, either based on observation of a recent activity, or a planned future activity. As we mentioned in a prior chapter, *inspection* involves the gathering of facts related to past events to help project future events. Inspection is necessary and all organizations do it. It is also typically a very formal process. Interestingly, inspection is almost always formalized, whereas coaching is often far less formal.

For example, in the case of one of our banking clients, we found that formality played into their sales managers' day-to-day job. When we encountered this client, they were very bullish on the formalization of their sales management activities. They called them "management routines," and they had very specific requirements for the execution of the meetings within these routines. On the surface, these routines appeared quite well designed. Closer examination, however, was quite illuminating.

The management routines consisted of the following types of interactions and associated descriptions:

- **Weekly sales activity reviews:** Meet with individual salespeople weekly to discuss their activities and results over the past week and their plans for the coming week.

- **Observational coaching:** Observe sales calls to assess and help develop specific behaviors and skills of the sales professional and to gather best practices to be shared with others.

- **Coaching:** Planned or scheduled coaching discussions that address or coach to a specific skill gap or promote skill enhancement.

- **Rounds:** Connect with sales professionals each day to determine how they're doing with their activities and goals.

- **Sales meetings:** Provide an opportunity to do one or more of the following:
    - Recognize and reward team members for their achievements.
    - Introduce new initiatives, product solutions, or innovations.
    - Identify problems and discuss solutions.

- **Monthly sales reviews:** Opportunity to meet with each sales professional to discuss the person's activity and sales results for the past month.

- **Quarterly performance reviews:** Opportunity to review with individual sales professionals their progress on their sales plan, to assess their performance against their performance management action plan, and to recommit to their sales goals.

- **Year-end performance reviews:** Year-end performance reviews that focus on individual sales professionals' progress for the year. This is an opportunity to celebrate the successes and accomplishments of the past year and agree to their overall performance to goal.

An initial perusal of the interactions within these routines leads one to marvel at the comprehensiveness of the approach. All interactions have a specific purpose and accomplish a necessary business outcome. Viewed together, these management routines seem to be a balance of coaching and inspection. However, the descriptions indicate that the balance is tipped in favor of inspection. Banks are very metrics oriented. This was certainly true of their management routines. As we mentioned earlier, activities are the only things that can be directly managed. These routines reflected a preponderance of activity *tracking*, not necessarily activity *coaching*.

Of the interactions included in the management routines, only two of them involved coaching. Unfortunately, the coaching interactions were the least formal of the lot. Every other interaction had specific time frames, agendas, and structures. Only the coaching interactions were left to the discretion of the sales managers. Although the coaching interactions had a *suggested* structure, they were at the *managers' discretion*.

> Inspection is often mandatory,
> whereas coaching is discretionary.

Managers conducted the mandatory interactions, and they rarely found time for the discretionary ones. Lots of activity was happening between the sales managers and the salespeople. It just wasn't *coaching activity*. The salespeople were being inspected to death and rarely coached. They were being inspected regarding their activity levels, sales results, overall performance to goal, and a host of other metrics. Managers were working hard, putting in long hours, and doing their best to meet the demands of their formal routines. The execution of these routines was unsatisfying for both the managers and salespeople alike. Compliance was high, satisfaction was low. Such is the nature of inspection gone wild. We feel busy. We're paying attention. We're just attending to the wrong things, or we're attending to the right things but in the wrong measure.

What the Research Says

Just how dangerous is an overemphasis on inspection? In our study of sales management coaching practices, we found a direct negative correlation between inspection and performance. Managers who do more inspection don't perform as well. Figure 6.2 illustrates that a full 75 percent of the managers in our study spent almost one-third of their scheduled coaching time *inspecting*. The top 25 percent of managers were *41 percent less likely to inspect* during scheduled coaching time compared with their lower-performing peers.

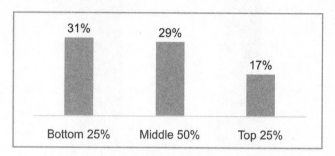

FIGURE 6.2 Inspection-Focused Interactions

Not only are high-performing managers significantly less likely to spend precious coaching time inspecting, they spend less time than their lower-performing peers doing forecasting and reporting. Figure 6.3 shows just how much less time high-performing managers spend on forecasting and reporting, which are nonrevenue generating administrative tasks. In his sales manager time study, Dr. Adam Rapp found a direct negative correlation between time spent managing information and manager performance.* The more time spent doing things like forecasting and reporting, the lower the manager's performance.

So, a few key trends of note. High-performing managers spend less time in their scheduled meetings focused on interactions that are nonrevenue producing. They spend less time inspecting and less time forecasting and reporting. Scheduling *coaching* discussions is an important first step, but what happens within those scheduled discussions matters. In later chapters we will provide very specific guidance on how to structure scheduled coaching discussions for maximum impact, including topics, frequencies, and durations exhibited by the highest-performing managers.

---

* Adam Rapp with Doug Hughes, Andrew Peterson, and Jessica Ogilvie, "A Question of Productivity and Performance: The Selling Sales Manager or the Managing Sales Manager?" Thought Leadership on the Sales Profession Conference, Harvard University, June 5–6, 2012.

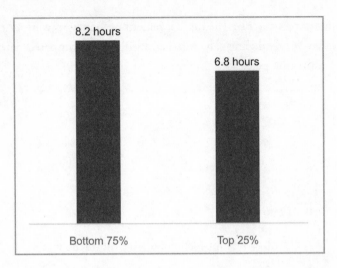

FIGURE 6.3 **Hours per Month Managers Spent Forecasting and Reporting**

THE RHYTHM TO FORMALITY

Formality is important, but it can be tricky. Too much formality and you paralyze your ability to coach and your salespeople's ability to sell. Too little and you leave salespeople unattended and confused, and you leave too many things to chance. So, what is the right balance? Why should you care?

Spans of control are increasing. Managers are managing more salespeople than ever. Managers are also faced with higher administrative burdens and increasing revenue targets. This is all happening while the percentage of sellers at quota is at an all-time low. Something needs to give.

In our four-year study of sales management practices, average quota attainment was 52 percent. Slightly more than half of the sellers in our study were at quota. The average reporting ratio was 8.9 sellers per manager. If there has ever been a case for prioritization, it is now. Managers know this intuitively—they just don't know what to do about it. Jack did. Jack established a management rhythm, a cadence for the most important interactions he needed to have with his team.

A *management rhythm* is the pattern of formal and informal interactions a manager engages in to advance sales efforts and achieve sales goals. This definition seems simple. Yet this important task of implementing successful management rhythms is a major failure point in most organizations we encounter. One important consideration that drives success or failure of a management rhythm is the sheer volume of formal coaching interactions sales leaders establish for their frontline sales managers.

> **Management rhythm:** The pattern of formal and informal interactions a manager engages in to advance sales efforts and achieve sales goals.

Overengineering: How Good Intentions Can Go Awry

In many of the organizations we work with, we encounter very formal management rhythms. In fact, the majority of organizations we encounter have them. Establishing a formal management rhythm is the new hot topic for improving a sales force. Everyone is jumping on the bandwagon. The problem is that they are jumping on the wrong wagon.

Whenever organizations attempt to formalize something without truly understanding *what* they are attempting to formalize, they get it wrong. And they typically get it wrong by *overdoing it*. The overengineering of management rhythms is so pervasive it deserves a closer look at how and why it happens.

We'd like to share a story about Dan: a smart, well-liked, and charismatic leader. He shot like a cannonball up the sales ranks at a high-tech infrastructure company. When we met Dan, he was the vice president of sales. We'll tell you more about him shortly. First, let us give you the backstory. We were brought into Dan's company by a savvy director of sales operations, Doug, who knew from vast experience that the sales management team was unlikely to achieve the desired growth goals using their current practices. This is not a new story, or an uncommon one—just a troubling one.

Dan's company had a tenured sales team. These folks had been around for a long time, through the heyday of growth. Selling for this company had been a good gig for many years. They grew so fast that they could pick and choose their clients. But then the growth slowed. It slowed to a crawl. The low-hanging fruit had all been picked. And leadership was worried. Everyone was worried—including the salespeople.

The sales operations director, Doug, had seen this same predicament play out in a variety of companies. He knew that any real change must happen on the front line. The salespeople had to adapt the way they sold. They would have to dig deeper into their accounts, expand their reach into other divisions, and interact with departments outside their comfort zone. This was a big change, and a scary one. Maybe not everyone would make it. Well, Doug would do his level best to equip the organization for change. And he would do it methodically.

When we met Doug, he was about three months into a very thorough analysis of seven different training companies, including ours. The interesting thing about him was that he'd already concluded that his change efforts needed to focus on frontline sales managers. Doug knew that the sales managers had to change the way they managed their sales teams. He knew that training was going to be a key enabler of this change. He wanted training that was specifically designed for sales managers and geared toward the types of guidance and coaching needed to drive significant changes in salesperson behavior. Because this type of training was not commonplace, it forced Doug to cast a broad net in his search for a solution.

Many companies—his included—tend to invest heavily in methodology, training, and tools to improve the effectiveness of their salespeople, yet they rarely get the desired lift in performance. Doug's company had invested heavily in a robust sales methodology. This methodology was quite clever and had sexy tools, exactly none of which were being used. Doug was jaded by the plethora of sales methodologies that had crossed his desk and drained his budget. Now he intended to focus his efforts on a different lever, the frontline sales manager. We helped Doug complete his analysis of sales management training options. We even helped him present his results to senior management, including Dan.

Although Doug's analysis was the most thorough we had ever seen, it left Dan nonplussed. Dan didn't disagree with the premise that frontline sales managers mattered and needed to be trained. He just didn't have faith that the training would result in any meaningful change in sales manager behavior. He was almost aggressive in his disbelief in the capabilities and motivation of his frontline sales managers. We walked away from the meeting a bit disheartened and, quite frankly, a little sad for Doug. Although Doug had worked very hard, his thorough analysis and the associated recommendation had met with a decidedly cool reception. Yet somehow, he seemed unaffected by Dan's response. When we followed Doug back to his office for a quick debrief, he shared the rest of the story.

Apparently, Dan had reached a similar conclusion regarding the importance of frontline management. Dan was all too aware of the decline in business and the implications for the company's financial health. Dan was so concerned that he had spent the better part of six months developing what he felt was the solution to the problem. Doug handed us a hard copy of Dan's *Leadership Playbook*. we read it from cover to cover and then put it down, with a big sigh. Ugh.

The Birth and Death of Dan's Playbook

Dan's work of art, his *Leadership Playbook*, was a testament to formality. His goal was to assemble a best-of-breed playbook for effective sales management. Dan had analyzed his business and come up with a plan for good management. Dan detailed the types of meetings he wanted his managers to conduct, including associated planning expectations. The following brief descriptions represent the eight types of interactions included in the playbook:

- **One-on-ones** (every other week): The manager and seller were to discuss individual opportunities within the pipeline. Progress was evaluated for each opportunity, including a review of recent activity and plans for upcoming activity. For each opportunity, a formal opportunity plan was to be completed. Opportunity plan templates were located within the CRM system and aligned to the company's sales methodology. The template was the vehicle that manager and seller used to discuss each opportunity and make any necessary adjustments. Opportunity plans were to be updated at the conclusion of each one-on-one. One-on-ones were approximately one hour.

- **Account reviews** (quarterly): These meetings included a strategic review of existing and targeted business within each major account. Each salesperson had at least five accounts that warranted this level of planning. Account plans were to be completed using the company's template and reside within the CRM system. Each account plan was to be updated immediately after the account review and then monthly thereafter. Account reviews were two to four hours in length, depending on the number of relevant accounts being discussed.

- **Territory reviews** (twice yearly): The first territory review occurred in the first month of the new fiscal year, and it included a review of the coming year's territory business plan. The territory business plans were to be completed using the company template. After six months, the second territory review was to be conducted to evaluate progress against the plan. The territory plans were to be updated immediately after each territory review. Each territory review was approximately two hours in length.

- **Pipeline updates** (weekly): Managers were required to submit a weekly forecast. The weekly pipeline updates provided the details managers needed to scrub each seller's pipeline and prepare the forecast. The weekly pipeline updates took approximately 20 minutes per salesperson.

- **Monthly field rides:** Managers were required to spend one day per month in the field with each salesperson. During field rides, managers were to observe sales calls using the company's behavioral coaching template. This template aligned with the company's sales methodology. Field rides were between a half day and a full day in duration.

- **Team meetings** (monthly): These meetings would be used for company and product updates as well as general communication with the team. Team meetings were approximately one hour.

- **Regional forecast calls** (weekly): All sales managers in the region shared their individual team's 30-day rolling forecast. They detailed which deals were to close, by which date, and the associated revenue amounts. All managers within the region had to attend. Regional forecast calls were approximately 60 minutes in duration.

- **Regional business reviews** (quarterly): In these quarterly meetings, each manager within the region provided updates on team performance against key metrics, raised any concerns with their progress, and revised their plans to reach goal. The estimated time needed for regional business reviews was approximately two hours.

After I (Michelle) reviewed Dan's *Leadership Playbook*, I said to Doug, "Wow! This is thorough. It's detailed, well thought out, and completely unrealistic." I asked him, "What happened when the playbook was launched?"

"Absolutely nothing," he replied. I admit, I was not surprised by the outcome. I have seen many versions of Dan's playbook in my career, and almost none of them have lived far past the launch meeting. Very little adoption. Almost no change. Why? Nothing in Dan's playbook was wrong. There was justification for everything he was asking sales managers to do. All of it made sense. It was just too much. A good idea run amuck. Let me explain.

Too Much of a Good Thing

Why the disconnect? It's rather simple: Dan, like many other playbook aficionados, assumed that a sales manager's time is discretionary. It is not. Dan assumed that sales managers get to choose how to allocate their time and effort. They do not. While it is certainly desirable, it is not factual. Managers do have some discretion about how to spend the 32 percent of time they have to manage their salespeople, but they are often ill equipped to make the best decisions.

Even if Dan's sales managers could make perfect time allocation decisions, they still couldn't implement his playbook because it was crafted under the wrong set of assumptions. It was designed to operate under *optimal* conditions, conditions that would allow the sales managers more than 32 percent of their time to devote to the team. The playbook was crafted for a world that doesn't exist. It simply ignored the 200 e-mails per day and other administrivia that are crushing the sales manager. Unfortunately, it didn't work in their environment. In fact, it couldn't work in their environment—not their *real* environment, the one they faced each day.

> Most leadership playbooks fail because they are designed for optimal conditions. Sales managers never work in optimal conditions.

GETTING ON THE RIGHT PATH

The hardest part about helping Dan improve the lot of his sales managers was helping Dan get out of his own way. Helping him see past the desired utopia, to the day-to-day realities that existed in his sales force. In today's world, sales managers have limited discretionary time. How they choose to use that time matters.

We helped Dan identify the few types of interactions his managers could have with their salespeople that would have the *biggest impact*. That was hard for Dan. He wanted it all. He couldn't *have* it all. He had to come to terms with the *possible*, which would consist of *small changes* in management discipline focused on the right things. His ultimate mandate had many of the excellent attributes of his first playbook—just fewer items, in more depth, focused on those critical few interactions that would make the biggest difference.

Dan's story is not uncommon. Lots of sales leaders have developed their own beautiful and utterly unfeasible playbooks, either on their own or with the help of highly trained consultants. Many unfortunate sales managers have tried bravely, and failed spectacularly, to implement such playbooks. What they don't realize is that moderation matters. Selecting the most important types of coaching conversations and formalizing *those* conversations is the key to operationalizing coaching into a manager's day-to-day job. For a robust example of the development of an overengineered playbook and how this unfortunate situation unfolds, please visit our website at www.vantagepointperformance.com/crushingquota.

The Minimum Level of Rigor Versus the More Button

So why is moderation an important consideration when developing the right rhythm of coaching? As we've already established, the sales managers' job is chaotic. Much of their day, and many of their choices, are outside their control. This isn't the way it's meant to be; it's just the way it is. Leaders don't like it. Neither do sales managers. Unfortunately, the problem is thorny, and neither faction really knows how to solve it. As we mentioned in the second chapter of this book and earlier in this chapter, Dr. Adam Rapp discovered that frontline sales managers only spend about 32 percent of their time managing their team. The other 68 percent is spent doing all of the other stuff, like reporting, forecasting, administration, and putting out fires.

The 32 percent of time managers have to manage their team members includes field time, coaching time, joint sales calls, strategizing opportunities—all of it. This is the heart of the disconnect between Dan's playbook and the reality of frontline sales management. This is the reason *coaching* isn't happening. This is the reason *rep development* isn't getting done. Managers have precious little time to spend with their salespeople, and most of that time is spent chasing and closing deals to hit their targets.

To make this more tangible, let's return to our sales manager Jack. Recall that Jack managed a team of 12 salespeople that spanned two provinces within Canada. That is a lot of people and a large geography. So how did he do it? How did he manage to have consistency in his approach to coaching his team? We all know how chaotic life is for sales managers, so what was Jack's secret?

Jack had figured out the minimum level of rigor needed to effectively manage his team. Recall that Jack conducted one-on-ones once per month with each of his salespeople. It would have been possible for Jack to conduct more frequent one-on-ones, say twice per month, but that would have been a stretch. Jack preferred to do his one-on-ones in person because he often scheduled field time to coincide with the one-on-ones. This allowed Jack to do the strategic work in the office time and the more tactical work in the field.

We asked Jack how he arrived at his current frequency of one-on-ones. He candidly shared that he had tried doing them more frequently, but he often had to cancel or reschedule them. It was creating stress and undue complications when his schedule was a constantly moving target. After about six months of constant rescheduling, he changed his scheduled one-on-ones to once per month. He felt that monthly one-on-ones were sufficient to accomplish the coaching needed to keep the team on target. For Jack, more was not better.

Jack had figured out what we were able to uncover through our research. The most successful sales managers don't coach more than their less successful peers. In our initial analysis, we found that the lowest-performing sales managers reported the largest number of coaching hours. There was a negative correlation between hours spent coaching and percentage of salespeople at quota. We thought this was strange—it seemed counterintuitive, yet there it was. Because this finding was so counter to conventional wisdom, we continued to examine our data.

When we analyzed this seeming anomaly a bit differently, something interesting came to light. Upon further analysis, we found that the most successful sales managers provided a moderate amount of coaching whereas the low performers tended to gravitate toward the extremes. Figure 6.4 illustrates this finding.

It makes sense that very little coaching would impede success; however, it is less obvious why *more* coaching would hurt performance. This is a little harder to grasp. Poor performers don't actually coach more, although they *think* they do and they *report* that they do. Poor performers have conversations with their salespeople more often, and those conversations are of shorter duration. This frequent, but superficial approach to coaching does not get to the depth needed to improve salesperson performance.

The best way to illustrate this point is to return to our exercise analogy. A well-designed and well-executed exercise plan often requires less time in the gym, and it yields better results than a haphazard plan. With

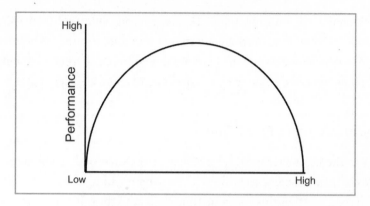

FIGURE 6.4 **Coaching Hours per Month**

focused effort, we could gain more benefit from three very targeted exercise sessions as opposed to five sessions that have no real focus. Effort expended does not necessarily equate to results. More exercise is not better. In fact, muscles need an opportunity to heal in order to build.

More coaching is not better, but the right kind of coaching, in moderate quantities, leads to better outcomes. In our research we found that regardless of the type of coaching, high-performing managers coached less frequently but for longer durations than their lower-performing peers. They were more focused and deliberate in their coaching interactions. Because they tended to hold less frequent coaching discussion with their salespeople, these high-performing managers *perceived* they were doing less coaching than their lower-performing peers.

> More coaching is not better. The right kind of coaching,
> in moderate quantities, leads to better outcomes.

Although it is highly possible that high-performing managers spent fewer hours coaching, one thing is certain: the coaching they provided was more targeted, more effective, and led to higher salesperson performance. This type of insight is only possible if one digs beneath the surface of hours spent coaching. The total number of hours a manager spends coaching is a very blunt measure. The more important insights are gained by examining *how* managers spend those hours and how those choices relate to performance. Those insights are shared in the chapters that follow and relate to very specific types of sales coaching and associated practices.

Moderation and Field Time

OK, so the most successful sales managers spend a moderate amount of time coaching as compared to their lower-performing peers. You may be wondering whether this coaching time is spent in the office or in the field. In our research we examined the many different types of sales coaching, including the amount of time managers spent in the field with their salespeople. Our findings, again, were surprising. They point to the minimum level of rigor and go against conventional wisdom.

Figure 6.5 shows what our research revealed about the correlation between field time and performance. The least successful managers reported the highest amount of time in the field. In fact, the lowest-performing managers consistently reported that they spent more time in the field than their organization required. The highest-performing managers reported spending the amount of time in the field that their organizations required or slightly less.

Again, we have a finding that is counterintuitive. How could this be? How could more field time impede performance? Well, time in the field

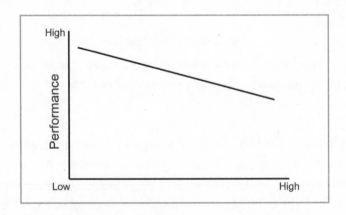

FIGURE 6.5 **Time in the Field and Performance**

can involve coaching, but more often it involves *joint selling*. When a sales manager is selling, it is difficult to be in the dual role of coaching. Even if a sales manager is coaching during field time, observing sales calls and providing feedback is only one type of coaching among many. Since higher-performing managers attend fewer sales calls, they orient their coaching to other types of discussion that happen in the office as opposed to the field.

You may be curious to see how this trend toward reduced field time jived with our sales manager Jack. Jack had figured out how to moderate the one-on-ones that happened in the office, but did he also display the reduced field time we found in our research? Jack's goal was to spend one day every other month in the field with each salesperson. So, six days of field time per year with each salesperson. This *every other month* field time fell below the company's desired targets; however, this frequency allowed Jack the flexibility to attend key sales calls that were outside of his normal rotation.

Did Jack spend less time in the field than his colleague Ed? Maybe. What we knew for sure was that his time was intentional and well planned. Could Jack have spent more time in the field with each of his salespeople? Could he have spent one day per month in the field with each of his salespeople as opposed to every other month? Maybe, but unlikely. If he had tried, he would have failed. Moderation strikes again.

Had we followed Ed's and Jack's career progressions, it is likely that Ed remained a sales manager and Jack ascended the ranks of sales leadership. Managers like Ed don't get fired. They get stuck. Managers like Jack get promoted because they know how to lead, not just sell. Jack provided leadership every time he coached one of his salespeople. Jack not only led but he also helped build future leaders by example.

What This Means for Our Coaching Efforts

This forced choice toward the minimum level of rigor goes against everything we've been taught as salespeople, athletes, and overachievers of every ilk. More is better! Until it isn't. We are told to not just set goals but to set stretch goals. When we think we can't do any more, we are told to do more. Take that extra step, run that extra half mile. Suck it up, buttercup. No pain no gain. And so the story goes.

Any manager who is trying to do it all is probably not doing any of it well. She is probably demoralized and defeated and wishes desperately that there were a few more hours in each day. She longs for a way to *do it all*. The liberating thing, the shocking truth, is that she can't. There is never enough time for a sales manager to do all the things that need to get done.

The most effective sales managers, the ones who survive and thrive in the job, have learned to prioritize their coaching efforts. They say yes to some things and no to many others. They are maniacally protective of their time and effort. How do we know this? Try distracting one of them. Try invading their team meeting with an overview of a new initiative. Try pulling them into a new pet project. They may participate, but only if it furthers their agenda to improve their team and hit their number. These high-performing managers are laser focused.

The hard message, the counterintuitive message for sales managers and sales leaders is this: small changes have big impacts. If they are the right changes and implemented the right way. We could go as far as to say, "Big changes have small impacts." Big changes make us feel like we are doing something meaningful, something important. Small changes make us feel like losers, like we're not really living up to our potential. They feel that way for a while, until we realize they are working. Then the epiphany comes. We realize we've made progress—genuine, sustainable progress. Now that is satisfying, both at the top line and the front line.

> **Big changes make us feel like we are
> doing something important.
> Small changes make us feel like losers,
> like we're not really living up to our potential.**

KEY TAKEAWAYS:
FORMALIZING SALES COACHING
INTO YOUR DAY-TO-DAY JOB

- Hitting your sales targets does not ensure effective coaching. Looking beneath the surface, formalization matters.

- Coaching happens on a continuum of formality. Ad hoc is the least formal and least effective. Scheduled is the most formal and drives consistent coaching practices over time.

- As-needed coaching discussions are more effective than ad hoc, particularly if they are planned. Finally, scheduled and recurring coaching conversations are the most formal, and they drive consistent coaching behaviors over time.

- Formality does not always lead to effective coaching. Inspection tends to be formalized, and coaching is often left to the managers' discretion.

- Management rhythms ensure consistent coaching practices. Over-engineering is the most common failure point that impedes development and adoption of effective rhythms.

- Sales managers should target the minimum level of rigor in their management rhythms to get the job done. The most successful sales managers coach fewer hours and spend less time in the field than their less successful counterparts.

- Small changes in coaching practices can have big impacts, if they are the right changes implemented the right way.

PART III

COACHING TO ACTIVITIES: THE ITTY BITTY NITTY GRITTY

CHAPTER 7

TERRITORY AND

ACCOUNT COACHING

Up to this point, we've made the case that coaching to activities matters. We provided empirical evidence that coaching to activities is the *only* type of coaching that positively affects quota attainment. We provided a framework to identify which activities, for a given role, are most likely to lead to desired outcomes. We've explored ways to ensure that the coaching conversations you have with your salespeople are structured for maximum impact. We've even delved into the idea of rhythms and coaching consistency. We've provided the building blocks you need to establish highly effective sales coaching practices.

Now, we dive into the specifics of the two sets of sales activities that are necessary for finding, expanding, and retaining business: territory management and account management. Territory and account management are similar in that both processes are designed to ensure that salesperson effort is applied in the most appropriate manner for maximum return. *Territory management* is designed to help salespeople properly apply effort *across many accounts*, whereas *account management* is about applying effort most effectively *within an account*. We will explore the typical activities within each process, best practices, and typical failure points. We will examine tools, rhythms, and real client examples for each process.

TERRITORY COACHING

The goal of territory coaching is to ensure that your salespeople target the right customers and prospects and attend to them with an appropriate level of effort. We liken territory management to our exercise analogy used throughout this book. Prioritize and exercise the right muscle groups and you get excellent results for effort exerted. Approach your exercise in a less structured, more haphazard way and results will be far less impressive. In fact, you might get frustrated by how hard you are working at your fitness and how meager the outcomes you experience. It is quite possible to expend the same, or even less effort, in a more targeted way and experience superior outcomes. The goal is to achieve the *maximum return on effort*—whether managing your fitness or mining a territory.

If we continue with our fitness example, we need to make the best possible decisions about which plan is the best plan to maximize the impact of our effort. The decisions we make about which types of exercises to do and in which frequency will ultimately determine the specific outcomes we enjoy—whether it be increased muscle mass, improved cardiovascular fitness, or even weight loss. It is the same with territory management and coaching. Our ability to help our salespeople make the best decisions about how and where to apply their selling effort will set them up for the most effective sales execution. We examine the more strategic element of territory coaching first, and then we dig into the tactical execution of the strategy we've helped our salespeople develop.

The *strategic elements* of territory coaching are reflected in the dark boxes in Figure 7.1. These are the three decision-making elements that set your salespeople up for success. The first of these elements, establishment of a *prioritization scheme*, is the primary decision that drives the rest of the territory management process.

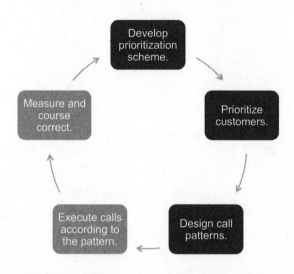

FIGURE 7.1 Strategic Elements of Territory Management

So, just how important is prioritizing customers? Why go through all the effort? Why not just leave it to your salespeople to figure it out? All fair questions. After all, if the goal of territory management is to maximize the return on sale effort, is effort on a formal prioritization process *well spent?* Well, prioritization matters. A lot. Figure 7.2 illustrates just how important prioritization schemes are in getting more salespeople to quota. In our study, the percentage of high-performing managers who had a formal segmentation strategy in place was *significantly higher* than the percentage of average and low-performing managers. This speaks to the increased rigor with which high-performing managers create task clarity for their salespeople, particularly regarding *where* to apply their selling effort.

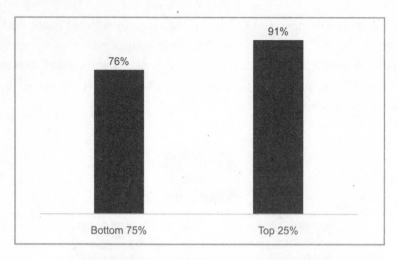

FIGURE 7.2 Segmentation Strategy in Place

Prioritization schemes do not have to be complicated, but they must be specific. The larger the organization, the more likely that the prioritization is done by either marketing or sales operations. In smaller companies, this prioritization falls on the shoulders of sales leadership, or in some cases, on the salesperson. Either way, the task must be accomplished, and the frontline sales managers' job is to enforce its application to the territories of the salespeople they manage.

Prioritization schemes can be as simple as an A/B/C/D designation, where A accounts have the highest potential and D accounts the lowest. Some organizations use a high-mid-low prioritization. The number of segments in the scheme should reflect the appropriate level needed to make a difference in effort applied. That is the whole point—to ensure that appropriate levels of effort are applied to different types of customers and prospects.

Figure 7.3 reflects an example of a prioritization scheme one of our clients used to segment and prioritize accounts. *Prioritizing customers* according to the scheme is a relatively straightforward task if the scheme is specific, well understood, and quantifiable. Salespeople within this organization had to use the segmentation scheme to prioritize the customers in their territory. Each account within the salesperson's territory fit into one of the four quadrants.

FIGURE 7.3 **Example of a Prioritization Scheme: Coverage Guidelines**

The client referenced in Figure 7.3 also set specific expectations regarding how often salespeople should call on each account. In this case, there were three separate types of sales roles within the organization, we'll call them roles 1, 2, and 3. Figure 7.4 reflects the targeted call patterns, per quarter, for each sales role by account segment. Although all three sales roles were responsible for covering many accounts, salespeople in

Role 1	
Maintain 2	Protect and Grow 4
Minimize 1	Discover 2
Role 2	
Maintain 4	Protect and Grow 8
Minimize 2	Discover 4
Role 3	
Maintain 6	Protect and Grow 12
Minimize 4	Discover 6

FIGURE 7.4 **Quarterly Call Frequency per Role**

role 1 had the most accounts, and salespeople in role 3 had the fewest. The call patterns were adjusted based on the breadth of account coverage.

Call patterns are identified to ensure that actual sales effort is aligned to desired sales effort. This last part of territory planning—the establishment of call patterns—is critical because sales managers must have some target to measure against. The action of segmenting accounts and establishing call patterns happens infrequently, usually yearly, and it is typically captured in a formal territory plan. Although most territory plans include these three elements, the plans themselves are unique to the organizations that design them.

In our study, over 75 percent of all managers required their salespeople to develop formal territory plans. The biggest difference between high performers and their lower-performing peers was the frequency of expected plan updates. High-performing managers required monthly updates to territory plans. Average and low-performing managers were more likely to require quarterly updates. This is an interesting finding because planning expectations put the accountability where it belongs, with the salespeople. High-performing managers ensure that their salespeople keep abreast of changes in their territories and adjust the prioritization of accounts accordingly. This ensures that selling effort is attended to and accounted for on a more consistent basis.

The development of territory plans is a very important strategic activity. It establishes parameters for how salespeople will attend to the accounts within their territory. The more *tactical* aspect of territory management and coaching is ensuring that calls are executed according to plan. Are salespeople adhering to the call patterns? Are they allocating more effort to high-potential accounts and less effort to less desirable accounts? It is the day-to-day execution that determines the efficacy of the plan. Like a good exercise plan, it is only as good as the degree to which it is followed.

Figure 7.5 reflects the more tactical and frequent elements of territory management and coaching, highlighted in the dark boxes of the diagram. The evaluation of *executed calls versus planned calls* is an ongoing process and very necessary to ensure territories are maximized. Salespeople are creatures of habit. They prefer to call on customers where the relationships are strong and avoid customers where relationships are weak or nonexistent. The more tenured the salesperson, the more common this trend. The most effective way to shift salesperson effort to the highest-potential targets is to pay attention to how their effort is expended—in a formal and consistent way. By formally *measuring* the calls salespeople make, managers can help sellers make needed adjustments and *course correct*.

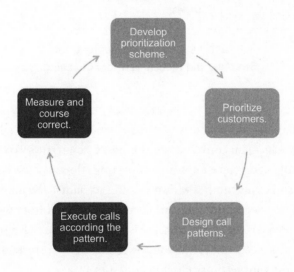

FIGURE 7.5 Tactical Elements of Territory Management

STRUCTURING TERRITORY COACHING CONVERSATIONS

The strategic and tactical elements of territory management benefit from coaching. Structure helps ensure that territory coaching effort is applied effectively. Strategic territory coaching ensures that a solid plan of execution is developed. Tactical territory coaching occurs to ensure ongoing execution against the plan. Although individual inputs, agendas, and outputs for the strategic and tactical coaching elements will vary by company, Figure 7.6 includes some of the more typical structuring elements.

Inputs	Agendas	Outputs
• Marketing lists • Prioritized account lists • Segmentation criteria • Activity levels • Pipeline by account segment	• Review prior month and/or quarter call patterns. • Determine impact of selling effort on pipeline. • Adjust targets and/or messaging. • Determine desired call cycles.	• Adjusted prioritization • Short-term target accounts

FIGURE 7.6 Structuring Elements for Strategic and Tactical Territory Coaching

To ensure collaboration, effective sales managers are prepared with good probing questions to drive a good balance of give-and-take during territory management conversations. In most cases, territory coaching involves helping salespeople improve prospecting efforts on new accounts as well as expand opportunities within existing accounts. The following lists of territory coaching questions can form a base to pull from when planning your own coaching questions. It is likely that you will also want to address some aspects unique to your own territory management process that will affect your territory coaching questions.

Prospective Accounts Questions

- In which segment of accounts have you had the most success generating interest?

- What messages are resonating? Which ones are not?

- For which accounts have you been unable to establish contact? What have you tried?

- Which competitors have a stronghold in your territory?

- Which competitors are you best able to unseat? Why?

- What have you done to differentiate our solutions in the minds of your prospective buyers?

Existing Account Questions

- Where have you had the most success upselling and/or cross-selling?

- When you've had success improving product mix and/or improving share of wallet, which strategies have you used?

- What have you done to reduce your service burden and create more selling time for your existing accounts?

- When you've lost share, which competitors have taken it? Why?

- Which accounts are at risk? Why?

- What plans do you have in place to mitigate these risks? How can I help?

Territory coaching, including prioritization, does not necessarily have to be driven from the top down. Oftentimes sales managers have to figure this out at an individual salesperson level. Regardless of the level of formality, helping coach your salespeople to focus on the customers with the highest potential pays off. For an example of an informal, yet effective territory coaching conversation, we return to a conversation that unfolded between our sales manager Nick and his salesperson Sarah. This conversation starts by examining activity levels. This question-and-answer section is an important tactical part of territory coaching; however, to get Sarah back on track, it quickly shifts to a discussion of prioritization.

EXAMPLE

Informal Yet Effective Territory Coaching Conversation

Nick: Sarah, let's review your recent activity levels. How many meetings have you been averaging per week?

Sarah: About 10.

Nick: Well, that is well below your target of 16 meetings per week. We will need to discuss how best to get you to your target. Meanwhile, let's take a closer look at the meetings you've been having and which customers you've been targeting.

Sarah: OK, sounds good.

Nick: I see that the majority of your sales calls have been on current customers with the strategy of upgrading some of their current solutions to newer products. Has that been your intention?

Sarah: Yes, I've typically had more success upgrading current customers than going after new business.

Nick: How about the competitive trade-in promotions we have for some of our products—like baffles and ceiling tiles? Which competitor has the most market share of these products in your territory?

Sarah: It has to be Relianz. They sell the lower end of each of these products, typically to the smaller businesses.

Nick: I wonder if it might be more effective to target Relianz customers and offer the trade-in incentives. What are your thoughts on that?

Sarah: Well, I have quite a large base of Relianz customers in my territory. I know who they are. I had some success with one of these accounts last month. I traded in some of their drop ceilings for our acoustic ceiling tiles, and the trade-in value we provided was impressive.

Nick: Think about the current customers you've had the most success with. Are they in a particular industry?

Sarah: Yes, they are. The older hotels and sports centers seem to be the most receptive to upgrading. The hotels typically have events happening simultaneously on multiple floors. The noise diminishes the client experience, and they lose repeat business as a result. The sports facilities have a similar problem with games happening on multiple floors.

Nick: So, would it make sense to narrow your focus to these two target groups that have good potential?

Sarah: That makes sense.

Nick: All right, what changes can you make to refocus your sales efforts to target those two groups?

Sarah: Well, I could spend half my time calling on Relianz customers about our upgrade promotions and the other half calling on my hotel and sports center customers.

Nick: I like that idea. What else can you do?

Sarah: I need to figure out what to say to get an appointment. I should come up with something that matters to each group of customers and demonstrates that I understand their issues. If I can develop some compelling messaging, it may help me increase the number of meetings I'm able to get.

Nick: I agree. That's a good start. I suggest you make a list of the Relianz accounts as well as your hotel and sports center customers. Then jot down a few items you think would resonate with each group. We can review the target list and the concerns you think we can address. Let's get together again on Friday morning at 8 a.m.

Sarah: Sure, I'll have my list and ideas about what to say to them by Friday.

Nick: Sounds good. See you Friday.

DEBRIEF

This territory coaching conversation between Nick and Sarah included all elements of territory management, both strategic and tactical. Nick began by examining Sarah's activity levels. He then moved to an exploration of Sarah's prospective customers to determine the best targets. Once they determined who the best prospects were, they shifted their focus to existing customers, narrowing Sarah's focus on the ones with highest potential.

Nick asked Sarah to think through how she would execute this new prioritized focus in terms of time management. In addition, Nick asked Sarah to think through a targeted message she could use to generate interest with some of her existing clients. One short conversation between Nick and Sarah covered all key elements of territory management. This is a prime example of how effective territory coaching doesn't have to be complicated. It just needs to be focused on the core elements of prioritization, allocation of effort, and relevant messaging.

ESTABLISHING A RHYTHM OF
TERRITORY COACHING

We've examined the inputs, outputs, and agendas for territory coaching, including an example of a robust territory coaching conversation. The next question to answer is how often you should have territory coaching discussions with your salespeople. Well, there are two different types of territory coaching discussions. There is the more strategic discussion of prioritization and then the more tactical discussion of call patterns. High-performing managers who focused their discussions primarily toward prioritization conducted these coaching sessions quarterly. High performers who focused their discussions on call patterns had those coaching discussion weekly. In other words, the more strategic the territory management topic, the less frequently it was discussed. Low- and average-performing managers were more likely to meet with each salesperson monthly, regardless of topic discussed.

All managers in our study, regardless of performance level, spent roughly one hour in each territory coaching discussion. The most prevalent topics for territory coaching were account prioritization, followed by call patterns, and finally targeted messaging to gain new customers. An interesting twist between formally scheduled and as-needed territory coaching had to do with the likelihood of coaching for targeted messaging to gain new customers. Managers who formally scheduled their territory coaching discussions were over *three times as likely* to discuss *targeted messaging* as compared to managers who used territory coaching as needed. This speaks to the link between formality of coaching and depth of coaching. Coaching to targeted messaging is much more detailed and tactical than coaching to prioritization or territory coverage.

Case Study: Strategic and
Tactical Territory Coaching in Action

This client was a healthcare company that employed several hundred territory salespeople. Each salesperson had a geographic territory that had between 150 and 250 accounts. The company was the market leader in its segment of the healthcare market. Only 29 percent of the client's salespeople were at quota. Margins were shrinking. New accounts were not being established at the desired rate. In addition, targets for expanded product mix and increased average selling price within existing accounts were not improving. Things were looking bleak.

Unfortunately, targets for new account acquisition and overall revenue growth were not being met. Leadership had to do something. The only way they could grow their business was to have the salespeople attend to their territories differently. Leadership put in place a requirement that all salespeople develop a formal territory plan by a specific date. All accounts within each territory had to be analyzed and placed in the appropriate segment. Evidence had to be provided to justify account placement within the prioritization scheme. Figure 7.7 includes guidelines for the territory planning process.

So, fast-forward, and all territories had been analyzed and territory plans developed and documented. Expectations were high for improved sales performance. Six months passed, and little progress had been made. The frustration grew. Again, very specific planning expectations were set and met. Every salesperson had a well-thought-out plan. What was happening here? Why such meager improvement?

There was a *tactical* element of territory coaching that was not happening. The development of territory plans was only the first step. The plans had to be followed, and they had to be executed. The sales managers were not evaluating the degree to which *planned effort* matched *desired effort*. Once salespeople developed their territory plans, the plans were promptly forgotten or ignored. There was no accountability for field execution.

The last and most important aspect of territory management and coaching is ensuring that salespeople do what they *say* they will do. The sales managers had to shift their territory coaching away from the strategic development of the territory plan, to the *tactical execution* of sales calls within the territories. This required a formalization of activity management within each territory. Managers had to inspect actual effort versus targeted effort and help salespeople more effectively target high-potential accounts. They needed to coach to the execution of the plans, and they had to do this on an ongoing basis.

Prioritize your accounts.	**Assumption 1: Targeting the right accounts to meet or exceed key performance indicators (KPIs) is a science.** The more rigorous that reps are about using quantitative methods for determining potential, the more likely they are to hit their KPIs.
	
	• Tools and methods for targeting and prioritizing.
	   • Account potential calculator
	• Quantitative filters to determine account potential:
	   • Prospects
	   • Existing customers
	• Qualitative filters to determine account potential.
	   • Account location, office characteristics

Align accounts against KPIs.	**Assumption 2: Mapping targeted accounts against specific KPIs is the shortest path to predictable growth.** • Tracking prioritized accounts in an organized way. • Changing and/or updating as new accounts are identified and other accounts fall off the list.
Determine call cycles and prioritize effort.	**Assumption 3: Calling on high priority targets in the right frequency with the right preparation will increase success rates.** • Call cycle for prospects and existing accounts. • How are current accounts prioritized? Do salespeople have different call cycles for low-, moderate-, and high-volume accounts? Is salesperson effort prioritized according to jobs and revenue? • What are the upcoming calls? How well are they prepared?

FIGURE 7.7 Strategic Territory Coaching Guidelines

These managers formalized tactical territory coaching discussions with each of their salespeople. Once per month they spent an hour examining the prior month's sales calls by account, as well as plans for upcoming targets. This held salespeople accountable because they knew their effort would be evaluated. Initially, this formal activity coaching was met with resistance. Salespeople had every excuse imaginable for why they couldn't spend more time prospecting new accounts. To ensure that prospecting efforts happened and were executed effectively, each monthly territory discussion included examination of accounts prospected, as well as plans to help salespeople conduct more effective prospecting calls in the coming month. Figure 7.8 includes an excerpt of guidelines the sales managers used when coaching their salespeople's prospecting activity. As you can see in the coaching guidelines, the coaching went beyond targeting

Conduct background research.	• Create a target list—housed on top opportunities report. • Research: website, drop by and talk to office staff, analyze geographical area, any history, local associations. • Research: review any available call notes in CRM from previous rep.
Get the meeting.	• Get the appointment. Build rapport with office staff and ask for appointment with doctor. • Goal is to get the meeting with the doctor. The meeting with the dispensary is the fallback.

Prepare for the meeting.	Explore current lab usage. Identify pain and gain points.
	• Pain points:
	  • Issues with current products.
	  • What are the biggest potential gaps based on what you found?
	  • What are your biggest challenges? What are your goals? How are you doing against those challenges?
	  • Look for the gaps and where you might be able to help.
	• Gain points:
	  • After pain is uncovered and expanded, the reps must explore what the customer wants to do about it.
	  • Potential needs—staff training, quality, product mix, lab, third-party plans, possible revenue goals.
	• Desired outcome:
	  • The goal of first meeting is to identify at least one area of potential interest and generate enough interest to get us in front of the owner.
	  • Target accomplishments would include a formal introduction with doctor and staff, learning the likes and dislikes of the previous relationship with our company, and securing a formal appointment for a second sales call.

FIGURE 7.8 Tactical Territory Coaching Guidelines: Prospective Account

to meeting planning. The sales managers had to help prepare their salespeople to successfully *get* meetings and then *conduct* them effectively.

To meet targets for improved product mix and average selling price, salespeople had to actively *sell* to existing accounts in addition to *servicing*. Salespeople had to break old habits of overservicing current customers and shift some of their effort to selling. Figure 7.9 includes an excerpt of coaching guidelines managers could use in their monthly territory coaching sessions to discuss selling efforts within existing high-potential accounts.

Identify the target.	• Identify **A** accounts for maximum share growth. This can be generated through the CRM.

Prepare for the meeting.	For each **A** account:
	• Get meeting with dispenser and owner to review job analysis, goals, and so on.
	• Understand criteria for lab selection. Which labs get what jobs?
	• The salesperson must provide value here. Discussion is more aspirational and gain based:
	  • Explore the value we have brought to the practice so the practice owner is very clear on this value. This sets the stage for us to earn the right to get additional jobs.
	  • Salesperson needs to have a candid conversation. Be up front, "I would like to gain more of your work. Here's the value I've brought to you."

FIGURE 7.9 Tactical Territory Coaching Guidelines: Existing Account

The territory coaching the managers provided was very specific and oriented toward obtaining and conducting effective meetings. The focus of the coaching managers provided regarding existing accounts was quite different from the coaching for prospective accounts, even though the process was similar. This was by design. This shift in behavior took time and attention. Sales managers had to be diligent and consistent in their attention to how seller effort was being applied.

Eventually the salespeople adjusted their effort. This was accomplished over time by ensuring consistent sales management attention to territory coaching. Some salespeople made the journey, but others did not. Sales managers had to assist their salespeople in making this transition, but it required a continued, diligent focus. So, what happened over time when managers put the right level of discipline in place for both strategic and tactical territory coaching? Things improved. Dramatically. Figure 7.10 shows the dramatic improvement in salespeople at or near quota.

In a little more than a year:

- Average selling price increased by nearly 10 percent.

- Product cross-selling improved by 44 percent.

- Percentage of sellers above quota rose from 29 to 49 percent, with another 25 percent near goal.

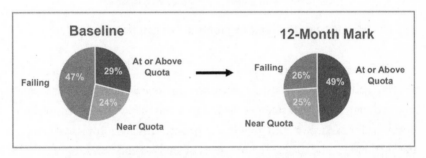

FIGURE 7.10 **Improvement in the Number of Salespeople at or near Quota**

ACCOUNT COACHING

Account coaching is the key to ensuring that your salespeople fully leverage their selling effort within a single large account. Accounts that warrant this type of coaching are strategically important to the organization, and they warrant focused, dedicated effort. Like territory coaching, account coaching has both strategic and tactical elements. Figure 7.11 indicates details for both the strategic and tactical elements of account coaching, with the more strategic elements indicated by the darker boxes. Account management and account coaching are very rich topics. This section provides a good grounding in the types of topics that must be addressed to effectively manage and coach to large accounts.

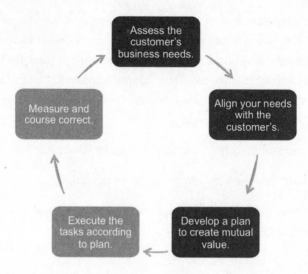

FIGURE 7.11 **Strategic Elements of Account Management**

The *strategic* elements of account management, and associated coaching, typically include some sort of *account assessment* or analysis. This analysis is designed to help salespeople identify the richest areas within those accounts for expansion and growth. Large accounts are complex, and navigating them can be tricky. The first level of analysis and coaching is to help your salespeople determine the lay of the land within the account. By analyzing how the account is structured, you can help your salespeople better target where, within the account, the opportunities are likely to reside.

Accounts have goals and objectives that change from year to year. These goals and objectives can form the best fodder for your strategic account coaching efforts. It is vital to ensure that your salespeople understand client goals and objectives, as well as any associated initiatives, because these initiatives will be top of mind for key contacts within the account. Initiatives are targeted both at the corporate level and at the business unit level. Initiatives are often put in place to address key business drivers occurring in the account's industry. Any *business needs* your salespeople's solutions address must somehow *align* to the achievement of account goals and objectives, as well as associated initiatives. This is the first order of business for your account coaching efforts—to ensure that your salespeople have a firm grasp of the account's strategic direction.

Another level of account assessment, and associated account coaching, involves identification of key decision-makers and influencers within the account. This must be done at the level in which your solutions are targeted. Helping your salespeople map out the relevant client contacts, their relative influence, and your salesperson's relationship with them is necessary before a pursuit strategy can be developed. It is likely that your salespeople have strong relationships with some key contacts and weak or no relationship with others. Helping coach your salespeople to navigate the host of players within the account is necessary to identify and cultivate additional opportunities.

EXAMPLE

Coaching Conversation Used to Leverage a Strategic Initiative

We offer a coaching example that leveraged a strategic initiative to improve our level of contact within an important account. One of our salespeople was frustrated with her lack of traction in a large global account. We had had several prior engagements with this client, but we had lost traction for any additional business. Our salesperson's key contact and internal coach had left the company, and she couldn't get traction with the new contact. An account coaching conversation ensued between one of our partners and the salesperson to improve our positioning within the account:

Coach: It seems like you have a good relationship with the director of learning, but nothing much is happening. You haven't been able to create any enthusiasm to do anything with their sales managers.

Salesperson: Yes, it is very disappointing. I spent two years building my relationship with the prior director, and then he left. The new person likes me, but she has no urgency to do anything new with the sales managers. She sees management training as a nice to have, not a need to have.

Coach: Well, what about the VP of sales operations. Didn't you have a pretty strong relationship with him?

Salesperson: Yes, he was our original executive sponsor, but he is very distracted. He is responsible for the successful implementation of their CRM system. They're in the middle of a Salesforce.com implementation. If it fails, he will most likely lose his job.

Coach: Well, that's interesting. Does he not see the link between the training we provide and adoption of the CRM system? In one of our other global client organizations, the VP of sales directly tied our management content to the launch of Salesforce.com. Every training event on the new system was tied to our management framework. The VP of sales was convinced this was the reason for such high adoption of the system.

Salesperson: Well, I guess I could try that. I don't really want to burden him right now. He's really stressed and worried about this implementation.

Coach: Well, does the director of learning see the strong connection between CRM adoption and our management framework? If she sees the connection, she can broach the topic with the VP of sales operations. If it comes from her, it might carry more weight.

Salesperson: Yes, I think that is the ticket. She likes me and is open to talking with me. Maybe you can help me come up with the best way to position our training in this new light.

Coach: Absolutely. I've done this before. All we need to do is identify the specific aspects of our management framework that help sales managers leverage CRM data to manage and improve sales performance. After all, that's the reason they buy CRM systems.

Salesperson: Yes, that's true. I think I can clarify this linkage for the director of learning and equip her to be my advocate. Do you think the VP of sales in our other client organization would be willing to talk to my VP of sales operations? You know, as a sort of testimonial.

Coach: Yes, I'm pretty sure he would. He's done that several times for us and seems very open. He's had success, so he's eager to talk about it.

DEBRIEF

In the above example, the salesperson was frustrated because she couldn't find a way to generate any additional business in a very strategically important account. Our training programs were not considered strategically important to either the director of learning or the VP of sales operations. This was our fault. Until we could find a way to connect our solution to a very high profile strategic initiative, there was no chance of getting back in front of the VP of sales operations. Once we made this connection, things turned quickly. We got back in front of the VP of sales operations and made it very clear how we could help him improve the success of the CRM launch. As a result, an urgent opportunity arose, and the training was quickly funded and contracted. Ahhh, the power of linking to client initiatives.

Most companies that have large, important accounts also have some sort of *documented account planning process*. Within that process, salespeople are expected to complete the plans with the help of their sales manager. This type of strategic account coaching ensures that the approach to a given account includes *alignment between your goals and the goals of the account*. In Figure 7.12, we offer a sample account plan for your reference. The analysis and associated *plan* become a targeting exercise, from which the salesperson can then execute a plan of action.

The *tactical* aspect of account coaching involves *execution of an action plan*. The action plan reflects a pursuit strategy for sales effort. In Figure 7.13, the dark shaded boxes represent those tactical elements of the account management process. The assumption is that you have coached the salesperson to help determine which areas within the account to target. Now, it is necessary to coach the salesperson on the best way to approach and pursue those targets.

Action plans include specific types of activities that must be accomplished, time frames for the execution of those activities, and resources needed to support those activities. The action plan forms the basis for ongoing tactical account coaching. As the salesperson executes the activities

Account Plan

Last update:

General Information

Customer name:
Account leader:

Primary Customer Contacts

Key contact: Function
                                relationship:

What We Want

                This Year   Next Year

Revenue:
Gross margin:
Share of wallet:
Installed products:
Strategic objectives:

What They Want

Strategic initiatives:
Stated needs:

Latent needs:

Issues to resolve:

Action Plan

Action Items	Owner	Completion Date
1.		
2.		
3.		
4.		

FIGURE 7.12 **Account Plan**

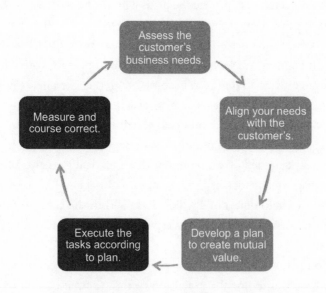

FIGURE 7.13 **Tactical Elements of Account Management**

within the plan, new opportunities should be generated. Strategies must then be developed to help salespeople navigate and win individual opportunities. As plans are executed and opportunities pursued, progress must be *measured* and *course corrections* must be made.

STRUCTURING ACCOUNT COACHING CONVERSATIONS

All account coaching conversations—whether strategic or tactical—benefit from structure. Strategic account planning conversations tend to be longer and more robust, whereas tactical account coaching discussions occur more frequently. The size and complexity of the accounts being managed will dictate the needed structure. Figure 7.14 includes some of the more common inputs, agenda items, and outputs for account coaching conversations.

Inputs	Agenda Items	Outputs

• Existing account plans
• Account-level activity reports
• Pipeline by account and/or product
	• Review account trends:
	  • Product penetration
	  • Share of wallet
	  • External influences
	• Develop strategy for account growth and/or retention.
		• Adjusted account plans
		• Action plans

FIGURE 7.14 Structuring Elements for Strategic and Tactical Account Coaching

To ensure that account coaching is highly collaborative, it is necessary to plan and use good account coaching questions. Both strategic and tactical account coaching benefit from collaboration. The following lists of account coaching questions can form a base to pull from when planning your own questions. Although these lists of questions are directionally correct, it is likely that you will have additional, unique aspects to your own account management process that will affect your account coaching questions.

Strategic Account Coaching Questions

- Which business units are the best targets for growth within the account?

- What are the account or business unit objectives? How have they changed year over year?

- Are there key initiatives in place that we can link into with our solutions? Who owns the initiative? What are the critical success factors for success of the initiative?

- Who are the key decision-makers and/or influencers in this business unit? What is the strength of our relationship with each contact?

- Who within the account is most likely to be your advocate and/ or coach?

- Who are the strongest competitors within the account and/or business unit?

- What is our value proposition and our most significant competitive differentiators?

- Where are we vulnerable within the account? Where are we losing business or seeing a competitive threat?

Tactical Account Coaching Questions

- What is the contact strategy and time frame?

- What is our initial value proposition for this contact and/or department?

- Which of our resources can we bring to bear to add value for this contact?

- What are our biggest barriers to making traction with this contact?

- What proof sources can we bring to bear to generate interest with this contact and/or function? Do we have case studies that are relevant to this contact that we can leverage?

- Who else do we know within the account who can be our coach and provide inside details about this contact and/or function?

ESTABLISHING A RHYTHM OF ACCOUNT COACHING

In our research, we examined the practices managers were using to coach their salespeople on large accounts. Interestingly, our findings on the differences in account coaching practices between performance levels were not as significant as with other types of sales coaching. Although account planning tended to be very formal, account coaching was not as formal as we expected, particularly tactical account coaching.

Regarding account planning, over 90 percent of all sales managers who manage major account salespeople require formal account plans. The percentage of managers who require plans for *all accounts* is higher for high performers than for their lower-performing peers. This makes sense because salespeople who handle large, important accounts typically have very few of them. Plans were expected to be updated either monthly or quarterly, and there were no significant differences in planning expectations by performance level.

The most typical frequency of account coaching discussions was monthly. Durations were between one and two hours for formally scheduled account coaching discussions and between 30 minutes and one hour for as-needed discussions. This highlights the difference in richness and depth of coaching discussions that are formally scheduled versus as needed.

Regarding the topics managers discuss during their account coaching conversations, Figure 7.15 shows that high-performing managers are significantly more likely to discuss strategic account planning compared with their lower-performing peers, and this trend is reversed for tactical account planning.

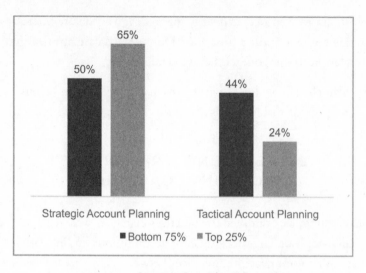

FIGURE 7.15 **Account Coaching Discussions**

When sales managers conducted account coaching primarily on an *as-needed* basis, they were three times more likely to focus their coaching on *account service issues*. That's a problem. Solving account services issues is important and necessary to retain business; however, it won't necessarily lead to *more* business. Account expansion requires strategic coaching and strategic selling. The less formal the approach to account coaching, the less likely managers are to focus their account coaching efforts on account strategy. This makes a very compelling case for increased formality in account coaching practices.

Case Study: Strategic and Tactical Account Coaching in Action

For this example, we return to our financial services client we introduced in Chapter 4. This real example provides rich detail on how this client approached both the strategic aspect of account management and the tactical aspect of executing action plans. Account and action planning may look different in your organization; however, many of the characteristics will be similar to the ones we share in the following example.

If you recall, client managers within this financial services company were responsible for managing up to 15 large existing client relationships. They retained and expanded these relationships by identifying and addressing additional areas of risk within the client's portfolio. Unfortunately, these client managers were spending more time servicing existing contracts than they were spending on expanding contracts into new areas.

In the early stages of our engagement, we worked with the client to identify the highest-impact sales activities necessary to drive the outcomes they wanted to achieve. These high-impact activities would be the targets for effective account coaching. Figure 7.16 identifies the results-objectives-activities linkage.

FIGURE 7.16 Results-Objectives-Activities Linkage

In this example, there were two high-impact activities that needed to be coached. Let's start with the first one, the proactive account analysis. Like many of our large clients, this client had developed a very rigorous process for account analysis. The client used a data-driven approach to analyze account usage against their existing contracts and identify areas for contract expansion. This analysis had to be completed by the client managers with the help of their sales managers. At the point when we engaged with this client, their analysis process was not being actively used. It was a great process, very thorough and effective, but not being used. The reason it was not being used was because the associated account coaching was not being done.

The account analysis portion of the process was very detailed and resulted in targeted expansion areas for additional service offerings. The account analysis involved three key *inputs*:

- **Client needs assessment:** A needs assessment conducted by the client managers with the clients to discover the client's business needs and objectives. In addition, the client manager and the sales manager had to research the account's performance through a review of their annual report and other relevant documentation. The outcome of the needs assessment was compiled into an internal briefing document for the account team.

- **Product penetration matrix:** Summary of current product and/or service penetration.

- **Performance survey results:** Customer satisfaction survey results.

After the initial account analysis, additional strategic account coaching took place in an *internal strategy meeting*. This meeting included the client manager, the sales manager, and the extended account team, and it was about two hours in length. The briefing document compiled by the client manager was one of the key inputs to this meeting. All members of the account team had to review this information prior to the strategy meeting. The *output* of the strategy meeting was a formal plan including a detailed analysis of key growth opportunities with supporting data, as well as a suggested agenda for a *formal meeting* between the key client contacts and the client manager.

The second high-impact activity was the formal meeting with the key account contacts. The goal of the meeting was to share the results of the account analysis and identify new opportunities for contract expansion. This formal meeting was incredibly important, and the work leading up to the meeting involved weeks of work and tremendous account coaching effort. This formal meeting where the client manager shared the results of the analysis and suggestions for contract expansion took place only once per year. Sales managers helped build out the agenda for the formal meeting and coached the client managers through the deeper preparation needed. This meeting was a sales call *on steroids*. If it was effective, opportunities would result. If not, well, nothing much changed.

Our client established specific rhythms for these internal strategy meetings, as well as standards and guidelines for the formal client meetings. The agenda for the *formal client meetings* contained the following items:

- Performance survey feedback from the client, with specific areas of suggested improvements

- Discussion of potential client needs based on thorough account analysis, details of how we can respond to needs with our products and services

- Agreement with client on which products and services to pursue further

This was a very detailed and formal account management process, with very specific coaching expectations and guidelines. As is often the case, even when the coaching process was formalized, adoption was not uniform across the organization. The earliest adopters were the highest-performing managers. As successes began to occur, adoption improved across the board. Within 12 months of launching the more formal activity-level standards and associated coaching standards, there was meaningful improvement in some of the client's key metrics:

- The percent of accounts penetrated with more than one opportunity increased from 59 to 77 percent.

- The percent of closed won opportunities increased from 42 to 52 percent.

The bottom line is that when sales processes and coaching are formalized, real improvement in execution takes place. Improved execution leads to improved performance—if the right things are being executed in the right way.

KEY TAKEAWAYS:
TERRITORY AND ACCOUNT COACHING

- The goal of territory coaching is to set your salespeople up for success by providing a way for them to prioritize customers based on potential, develop call patterns that differentiate level of effort by priority, and ensure that execution of calls is aligned to the call patterns.

- Managers who ensure that a segmentation strategy for customer prioritization is in place significantly outperform managers without this practice.

- Territory planning is a very formal process. The highest-performing managers require monthly plan updates.

- Structuring territory coaching leads to better performance outcomes. The most successful sales managers conduct strategic territory coaching quarterly and tactical territory coaching weekly. Territory coaching conversations are typically one hour in duration.

- Managers who formally schedule territory coaching conversations are three times more likely to coach salespeople on targeted messaging.

- The goal of account coaching is to ensure that your salespeople fully leverage their selling effort and associated outcomes within a single large account.

- *Strategic account coaching* involves analysis of accounts to include assessment of customer needs, alignment of the sellers' solutions to those needs, and a formal account plan to create mutual value.

- *Tactical account coaching* involves the execution of action plans, measurement of account progress, and course correction when needed.

- Over 90 percent of managers who manage major account salespeople require formal account plans. The highest-performing managers require account plans for all accounts.

- The most typical rhythm for account coaching is monthly. Durations are between one and two hours for formally scheduled coaching, and between 30 minutes and one hour for as-needed account coaching.

- The highest-performing managers focus on strategic account coaching; the lower performers focus on tactical account coaching. Managers who conduct as-needed account coaching rather than formally scheduled coaching are three times more likely to spend their coaching time discussing account service issues. This highlights the importance of formalizing account coaching practices.

CHAPTER 8

OPPORTUNITY

COACHING

Opportunity coaching is the exciting stuff. It gets our juices flowing and our wheels turning. It is where we can pull forth our own sales experience and use our knowledge to figure out how to compete and win deals. This is the kind of coaching we *love* as sales managers. We love it because it involves the most fun part of selling—figuring out the best game plan to beat the competition and win deals. We get to put on our strategy hat and, in the process, look smart. We really like that. We like that a lot.

Because we tend to like it so much, opportunity coaching is the most prevalent type of coaching sales managers provide. When we poll sales managers about the mix of different types of coaching they conduct with their salespeople, they overwhelmingly orient toward opportunity coaching. Opportunity coaching is fun, and it feels productive; however, few managers get this important type of coaching right.

In this chapter we offer research-based guidance on the nature of opportunity coaching, the types of activities managers can coach, and the specific practices utilized by the highest-performing sales managers. We examine the trajectory of opportunities from the perspective of the buyer, and we link salesperson activities and coaching recommendations to each stage of the buying process. In addition, we offer findings regarding the best structure, duration, and rhythms for effective opportunity coaching.

THE GOAL OF OPPORTUNITY COACHING

The goal of opportunity coaching is to help salespeople qualify, pursue, and win deals. The larger and more complex the products or service being sold, the more critical it is for managers to get this right. Why is opportunity coaching so critical? Because buyer behavior changes during the course of a buying decision. The more complex the buying decision, the more challenging the sale. In fact, in our study of management coaching practices, we found a negative correlation between the complexity of the buying task and the likelihood of salespeople making quota.

Complex solutions are harder to sell. In our study, the more complex the buying decision, the less likely salespeople were to make quota. Buying complexity accounted for 17 percent of the variation in quota attainment. This means that salespeople who sell solutions that are harder for buyers to buy are *17 percent less likely to make quota*. That's huge! Opportunity coaching matters, and the more complex the solutions sold, the more critical it is for managers to get this right.

Because the complexity of the buying decision has such a significant impact on quota attainment, we orient our guidance to the stages of the buying process. This is the best way to reduce the negative impact of buying complexity on deal pursuit.

So, why such an intentional focus on the buyer? Because salespeople and sales managers tend to view opportunities from the *seller* perspective. The reason this seller orientation is so pervasive is because this is the way they are trained to think. We obsess over the steps to the *sales* process, making sure they are well documented and adequately captured within the CRM. We make sure that our salespeople accomplish each step and provide evidence of their progress. Whenever we are presented with an opportunity management process—whether it is in a training program or within our own CRM system, it focuses on the *salesperson*, not the buyer.

Instead, to understand what salespeople and managers should be doing, we need to look at opportunities from the *buyer* perspective because they are the ones we need to influence.

COACHING ACROSS THE BUYING PROCESS

The initial goal of opportunity coaching is to determine whether an opportunity is worthy of pursuit. Is the opportunity desirable? Is it winnable? Does the salesperson have the time and resources to pursue it? These are all important questions that benefit from dedicated coaching. Salespeople tend to have an overly optimistic view of their chances of winning. In fact, salespeople are often willing to pursue deals that aren't winnable. As a sales manager, a vital part of your role is to ensure that your salespeople are spending their time wisely, pursuing deals they *can* win. Spending time pursuing deals you *want* them to win.

Once an opportunity is deemed worthy of pursuit, coaching is needed to ensure that the approach your salespeople take is aligned with the customers' buying process. Each stage along the buying process requires adjustments to the salesperson's approach. Figure 8.1 is an example of a typical buying process.

Identify Needs

In the identify needs stage of the buying process, buyers are figuring out whether they need to make a change. Buyers evaluate their current situation and determine if the upsides of making a change are worth the effort and expense involved in making the change. The identify needs stage is typically the longest stage and the most psychologically difficult for buyers

Identify needs.	Establish criteria.	Assess solutions.	Mitigate risks.	Decide.
Buyers examine their needs to determine if a change is warranted.	Buyers develop criteria they will use to evaluate various solutions to meet their needs.	Buyers assess solutions against their criteria to determine which ones are the best fit.	Buyers evaluate their risk in making a change to determine if the reward offsets the risk.	Buyers select their preferred solution.

FIGURE 8.1 **Typical Buying Process**

to navigate. Change is hard. People, including buyers, are not hardwired to change. Most of us prefer the status quo because it is familiar. Many a sales opportunity has languished because the salesperson thought the buyer had moved beyond this stage, when in fact he hadn't. Buyers typically decide to make a change only when the pain of staying in their current situation exceeds the pain of changing.

> **Buyers typically decide to change only when the pain of staying in their current situation exceeds the pain of change.**

Selling in the identify needs stage is oriented toward effective opportunity qualification. Salespeople must gain the right type of information to establish the viability of the opportunity. Determination of and getting access to the right level of contacts and exploring relevant buyer challenges is vital to building urgency and desire for change. Understanding how buyers make decisions, who is involved in those decisions, and typical time frames allow salespeople to better scope the trajectory of an opportunity. Salespeople must build buyer urgency by examining the downsides of staying with the status quo and exploring the upsides of making a change, from the buyer perspective.

Typical sales activities at this stage include these:

- Identify the steps of the customers' buying process.

- Identify key decision-makers and influencers.

- Uncover and assess buyer and/or business needs.

- Identify project budget.

Coaching in the identify needs stage ensures that salespeople conduct effective client research, objectively assess opportunity viability, and gain required information during individual interactions. Salespeople who don't obtain needed information lack the ability to properly qualify deals. As a coach, you must make sure that your salespeople gain access to all relevant decision-makers and influencers in order to qualify and shape the trajectory of an opportunity. Most deals are made or lost based on the salesperson's effectiveness at this early stage.

Typical *coaching errors* at this stage involve the assumption that salespeople know how to properly qualify deals and will do so consistently. This results in a tendency to wait until a deal has been deemed qualified before opportunity coaching is offered. In other words, managers wait to provide coaching until a deal is at the later stages. This is a dangerous trend. We have found that even very experienced salespeople omit critical information in their qualification process. Salespeople also tend to apply heavy effort to opportunity pursuit without getting into the specifics of whether the opportunity is real.

Establish Criteria

In the establish criteria stage, buyers are evaluating what is important to them in making a change. With any buying decision, certain things will be more important than other things. Buyers develop a set of criteria they will use to assess the viability of different solutions. Buyers who are serious about making a change will have a well-developed set of criteria.

As part of this process, buyers must decide which criteria are most important and which ones are less important. For example, the best solutions are often the most expensive, so solution quality and low price are often in conflict. Buyers have to make trade-offs. Buyers who are *kicking the tires*, so to speak, are often ambiguous about what is important to them. Lack of established buying criteria is a telling sign that a buyer is not serious about making a buying decision.

> Buyers who are serious about making a change will
> have a well-developed set of buying criteria.

Selling in the establish criteria stage is oriented toward understanding and shaping the criteria buyers will use to make their purchase decision. Gaining an understanding of the buying criteria must be accomplished through proper questioning. Salespeople must find evidence of buying criteria and the relative ranking of these criteria. Because buyers often struggle making trade-offs, it is vital that salespeople have a strategy to help buyers navigate this important task. It is impossible to develop a winning pursuit strategy without a clear picture of what is important to each buyer because different buyers will have different criteria. Salespeople often fall into the trap of assuming that the buyers' criteria line up well with their solution attributes. It is for this reason that getting tangible evidence of buying criteria is vital for all key decision-makers and decision influencers.

Typical sales activities at this stage include these:

- Identify potential return on investment.

- Identify buying criteria.

- Assess competitive landscape.

- Develop strategy to influence buying criteria to competitive differentiators.

Coaching at the establish criteria stage is oriented toward ensuring that salespeople truly understand and are prepared to shape the criteria the buyers will use to make their purchase decision. Gaining an understanding of the buying criteria must be accomplished through proper questioning, which you can help sellers develop through your coaching efforts. As a coach, you must require evidence that your salespeople uncover this information. It is extremely difficult and not particularly productive to develop a relevant strategy without this vital information. Different buyers will have different criteria, and some of their criteria may be in conflict. Coaching to help sellers uncover and influence buying criteria, as well as reconciling criteria across multiple buyers, is highly valuable. By adhering to a buyer focus during your coaching efforts, you can help your salespeople avoid the trap of solution bias. Your salesperson's solution is a good fit only if the buyer thinks it is a good fit. Case closed.

Coaching to ensure that sellers find out which competitors are being considered is also vital. Although your salespeople are influencing the way their buyers think, so are their competitors. Knowledge of the competitive landscape will affect which criteria the salespeople emphasize and with whom. Coaching in this stage can help the salespeople determine how to establish value and set themselves up for differentiation in later stages of the buying process. In some cases, if the competition is especially strong, an opportunity may not be worthy of pursuit.

Typical *coaching errors* at this stage involve *parochial bias*. We all believe our solutions are the best, and it is easy to assume buyers feel the same way. As a coach, it is vital that you gain evidence that your salespeople have uncovered the *actual* buying criteria that will drive the purchase decision. Often, the criteria buyers share are not at a sufficient level of detail to be useful. Helping prepare salespeople to dig beneath the surface and *quantify* buying criteria forces buyers to be deliberate about how their selection will be made. The most successful sellers do the best job shaping buying criteria and driving consensus across multiple buyers.

Assess Solutions

This is the stage at which buyers are digging into the details of various solutions and comparing them to the criteria they've established. Buyers are determining how each solution they are considering will meet their needs. This is a vital step in the buying process because buyers almost always consider multiple solutions from various providers. Their goal in this stage is to make the best choice—the choice that will best satisfy their needs. As buyers evaluate various solutions, their buying criteria often change. As buyers learn new information during this stage, that information often reshapes what they deem as important.

Selling in the assess solutions stage involves the position of solutions in the most attractive light, linked to established buying criteria. Salespeople must vet the buyers' perception of their solution, as well as the buyers' perception of other solutions under consideration. This is often a blind spot for salespeople. Salespeople are typically very biased toward the strength of their own solutions, to the point that they make assumptions about their buyers' perceptions. Salespeople are often shocked when they find out they are not the front-runner in any given opportunity. The only way salespeople can gain a true picture of the perceived strength or weakness of their solution is by getting this information from the buyers. These questions are sometimes hard to ask, and buyers can be hesitant to provide this level of detail for fear that they are exposing too much information.

> **Salespeople are often shocked that they are not the front-runner in any given opportunity.**

Typical sales activities at this stage include these:

- Determine solution scope.

- Develop formal proposal.

- Present proposal to key decision-makers.

- Establish return on investment.

- Refine and/or reinforce the buying criteria.

Coaching in the assess solutions stage is oriented toward helping salespeople position their solution in the most attractive light based on established buying criteria. Because a critical success factor at this stage involves the vetting of the buyers' perceptions, it is useful to play the devil's advocate during your coaching discussions. Salespeople must vet the buyers' perception of *their* solution, as well as the buyers' perception of *other solutions* under consideration. As a coach, you can help your salespeople look at the various solutions being considered from the buyers' perspective and the competitors' perspective. You can help your salespeople avoid being lulled into a false sense of strength by examining why their solution might not be strong and where the competitors' solutions may be superior. This thorough examination of solutions will help give your salespeople a more realistic view of their solution strength. It will also provide specific areas where your salespeople may need to further shape and influence specific buying criteria.

This stage often includes a formal solution presentation. Salespeople from the various solution providers are often invited to a live meeting to present their solution to a committee of buyers. It is at this point that buyers narrow the field and select the final few providers whose solutions are perceived as the best fit. This finalist presentation is an important opportunity for salespeople to establish additional value and shape buying criteria. Coaching is critical to prepare salespeople to effectively present their solution in the most compelling manner. I've been involved in opportunities where our solution was the front-runner going into one of these presentations, and we lost the deal. Our competitors did a much more effective job tying their solution to the buyers' criteria. It was a powerful lesson, and it dramatically affected our approach thereafter.

Typical *coaching errors* at this stage involve lack of diligence regarding the buyers' evaluation of the range of solutions being considered. It is easy to assume that your salespeople are in a position of strength if their solution seems to align best with the buyers' criteria. However, many a deal has been lost due to the strength of the buyers' relationship with another supplier. It is shocking how many tenured salespeople don't ask buyers how they rate the different solutions under consideration. It is not enough just to find out who else is being considered. Your salespeople must find out how those various solutions stack up in the mind of the buyers. As a coach, you must prepare your salespeople to gain this vital information and then develop a strategy to adjust perception as needed to improve competitive positioning.

Another common, yet almost unbelievable, coaching error is assuming that your salespeople know whom they are competing against in any given deal. We are often shocked by the number of times salespeople fail to even ask who else is being considered. It is very difficult to coach your salespeople on the best way to differentiate if you don't know the competitive landscape. Your buyers' choice of potential solutions is very telling and speaks volumes about how they are considering addressing their needs.

Mitigate Risks

In this late stage of the buying process, buyers have typically narrowed the playing field down to a single provider. Having decided which provider to choose, they turn their attention to other things. In the early stages of the buying process, buyers are thinking about what they want. They are considering all the ways their lives will be better by making a change. At this late stage, buyer thinking shifts dramatically. Buyers start analyzing what they stand to lose by making a change. They begin to evaluate what might go wrong, how this might turn out badly. Buyer goals at this point involve finding ways to minimize the risk of making bad decisions.

Selling in the mitigate risks stage involves the surfacing of buyer concerns, negotiation of terms, and development of implementation plans. Because buyers become insecure at this stage, the job of the salespeople is to find ways to reduce the buyers' perceived risks. This can often be accomplished through connecting your buyer with a satisfied customer to provide a proof source. It can also be accomplished by getting details of exactly what the buyer is worried about. It could be service levels or implementation support. Again, it is vital for salespeople to gain the real concerns and dig beneath surface-level objections. It is also important for salespeople to hold off on any type of negotiation until all buyer concerns have been addressed. Negotiation is not a substitute for good selling and should not be considered until all buyer risks and concerns have been mitigated.

> Negotiation is not a substitute for good selling and should not be considered until all buyer risks and concerns have been mitigated.

Typical sales activities at this stage include these:

- Uncover buyers' perceived risks.

- Provide referrals and proof of concept.

- Clarify buyer expectations and service levels.

- Negotiate and finalize terms and conditions.

- Establish implementation plan.

Coaching during the mitigate risks stage is oriented toward helping salespeople build buyer confidence. Buyers often become insecure during this stage, and salespeople must tread carefully. What is most interesting about this stage is that most salespeople don't plan for it. They don't expect it, even though it happens every time. The larger the decision, the thornier this stage becomes.

As a coach, it is vital to prepare your salespeople to effectively navigate this stage of the buying process. Effective coaching in this stage helps salespeople provide adequate proof sources, negotiate terms, and reinforce solution fit. A difficult aspect of this stage is that buyers often reduce the frequency and timeliness of their communication with salespeople. They become radio silent. Unfortunately, buyer silence often causes salespeople to become radio*active*—dramatically increasing their level of contact with the buyer. Badgering a buyer who is insecure is a recipe for disaster. Buyers tend to be very unpredictable at this stage. They can ignore salespeople for days on end, and then make an urgent request that must be met within an hour. Good coaching helps salespeople anticipate this type of erratic buyer behavior and handle it gently.

Typical *coaching errors* at this stage involve a tendency to assume that negotiation is the best risk mitigation strategy. As sales managers, we can be far too quick to reduce price, lower margins, and make concessions as the way to move a sale to successful close. Although most buyers will negotiate terms and costs, negotiation is not a solution to buyer concerns. Concessions should be considered only after all perceived risks have been addressed. Effective coaching at this stage helps salespeople understand

and apply the best approach to uncover and resolve buyer concerns and perceived risks.

WHERE TO APPLY YOUR COACHING EFFORT

We've just examined the stages of a typical buying process. We've provided guidance on buyer behavior during each stage, typical salesperson activities, coaching suggestions, and typical coaching errors. The next logical questions are these: "Of all of the stages I *could* coach, which *should* I coach? Are all buying stages equally important from a coaching perspective? How do I choose where to apply my coaching effort?"

In order to make this important choice of where to allocate your coaching effort, it is useful to conceptually divide a typical buying process into the early stage and late stage for coaching purposes. It is helpful to think about a buying process from this perspective because the salespeople's activities fundamentally shift when they transition from early to late in their opportunity pursuit. Coaching efforts should incorporate a similar shift in focus. As indicated in Figure 8.2, early-stage coaching efforts should help salespeople effectively *shape* deals by influencing buyer needs and buying criteria. Late-stage coaching efforts help sellers position their solutions in the most effective way to compete and *win* deals.

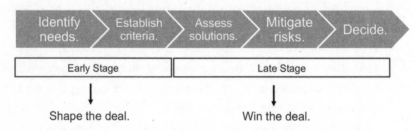

FIGURE 8.2 Early- and Late-Stage Coaching Efforts

The natural tendency for sales managers is to coach opportunities that are in the mid to late stages of the buying process, when the buyers are assessing options and negotiating terms. This seems intuitively correct because the late stages are where most of the action seems to happen.

Sales cycles heat up, buyer requests get more urgent, salespeople get anxious. Managers see these late stages as vital to the chances of winning a deal. And they are right. Salesperson effectiveness in the late stages is vital to competing and winning deals. However, counter to conventional wisdom, these late stages are not the ones that benefit most from coaching.

In our study of sales management coaching practices, early-stage coaching was significantly and positively related to higher performance—both from an overall revenue perspective as well as the percentage of salespeople making quota. The top-performing managers in our study overwhelmingly orient their coaching toward the early stage of opportunity pursuit. Figure 8.3 shows how much more likely high-performing managers are to focus their coaching on the early stage of the process as compared to their lower-performing peers. These early-stage coaching discussions are not as urgent as late-stage discussions; however, they are directly related to getting more salespeople to quota.

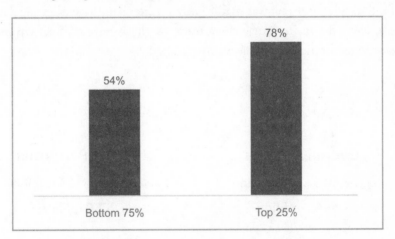

FIGURE 8.3 **Formal Meetings: Focus on Early-Stage Opportunities**

So why does this orientation toward early-stage coaching have such an outsize impact? Because sales managers who coach in the early stages of deal pursuit help ensure that the deals their salespeople pursue are real and winnable. They also tend to be very rigorous about ensuring that their salespeople are thorough in their qualification efforts. No budget? Not yet qualified. Not at the right level in the organization? Not yet qualified. No time frame for the project? Not yet qualified. No internal champion? Not yet qualified. Although different solutions have different key milestones at this stage, it is likely that you have a sense for what those milestones are that indicate successful qualification in your business.

Coaching in the early stage of opportunity pursuit will help your salespeople shape and pursue winnable deals. It will also increase the likelihood that they *will* win. Managers who are committed to early-stage coaching enjoy healthier pipelines and higher close rates. They help their salespeople get good deals in the pipeline and keep bad deals out.

It is always useful to examine how this trend plays out in specific organizations. It feels more real and less academic. Figure 8.4 shows the power of early-stage coaching as evidenced in one of our client organizations. The left-hand side of this chart shows average pipeline statistics across the entire sales management team. The right-hand side shows pipeline statistics for their highest-performing sales manager. The average pipeline size for the high performer was significantly smaller than the average pipeline size across the entire management team, yet the average sales per rep and close rates for his salespeople were much higher.

Overall Average

Average pipeline: **$41 million**

Sales/rep: **$4.7 million**

Highest Performer

Average pipeline: **$29 million**

Sales/rep: **$7.0 million**

FIGURE 8.4 **A Real Client Example Showing the Importance of Early-Stage Coaching**

So, what was the secret sauce of this high-performing sales manager? Why were his salespeople so much more productive than the norm? How could his salespeople produce so much more revenue with smaller pipelines? This high performer was maniacal about coaching to the early stages of his salespeople's opportunities. Although all sales managers in this organization had weekly coaching discussions with each of their salespeople, the high performer was the only one who focused his coaching effort on early-stage opportunities.

This manager rigorously questioned the viability of any given deal, digging into the details of opportunity to understand key players, business needs, budget, and timelines. He was also very specific about the requirements that had to be met for an opportunity to be put *into* a salesperson's pipeline. This was one of the primary reasons his pipelines were smaller and his win rates were higher. He didn't coach *more* than the other managers. He coached *differently*. He coached early and late—splitting his time effectively between the two. His lower-performing peers only coached late.

SALES PROCESS MEETS BUYING PROCESS

Recent research by SiriusDecisions indicates that buyers are engaging with salespeople later in their buying process than ever before. The proliferation of information available on the Internet has taken a lot of the power away from the salesperson and put it in the hands of the buyer. Buyers have ready access to details about our solutions and the solutions of our competitors. The most recent statistic is that buyers are 60 percent of the way through their buying process before they talk to a salesperson. If we line up the stages of the buying process and the sales process (specifically the opportunity management process), we see the disconnect depicted in Figure 8.5.

In this dangerous situation, salespeople have very little information about how the buyers have navigated their process thus far. Vital information has been considered by the buyers, but not with the help of the salespeople. Not with the help of *your* salespeople. Buying criteria have been established and ranked, and competitive solutions have been considered, and buyers are often shopping around for the best deal on what they've *already decided* they want. This is potentially crippling for salespeople.

Salespeople are very easily seduced by these types of situations because they have an interested buyer, one who has the intent to buy, a budget,

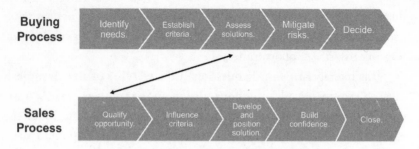

Buying Process

Identify needs. | Establish criteria. | Assess solutions. | Mitigate risks. | Decide.

Sales Process

Qualify opportunity. | Influence criteria. | Develop and position solution. | Build confidence. | Close.

FIGURE 8.5 **The Disconnect in How the Stages of the Buying and Sales Processes Line Up**

and most likely a time frame. This is the opposite of early-stage coaching because it is virtually impossible for salespeople to effectively shape the deal. It is already shaped, most likely by one of your competitors. This scenario often manifests as a request for proposal. The salesperson receives a request for proposal from a hot prospect. Wow, on the surface this seems like manna from heaven. But it really isn't. It is a slippery slope that can consume massive sales resources on a deal that has very little chance of ending in a win.

This situation screams for in-depth coaching—not necessarily on how to best win the deal but on whether to even pursue it. In most cases, if salespeople have not been involved at all in the shaping of the buyers' criteria, it is highly unlikely they will win the deal. This is particularly common when the prospects have a very strong relationship with their current supplier and have leaned heavily on that supplier to help them shape their desired solution. This information comes to light only when salespeople ask the right questions about which solution providers are under consideration, as well as the nature of the prospects' existing relationships with those providers.

Once buyers decide what they want, they feel they need to *shop around* and make sure they are making the best choice. We can't blame buyers for this behavior. We also exhibit this same type of behavior when we buy things. Unfortunately, understanding buyer behavior doesn't make this situation any less problematic.

Our company has gotten to the point that if we receive unsolicited requests for proposals from prospects we've not engaged with, we politely decline the invitation. Buyers don't like this type of approach, and can get quite indignant. For example, their official buying process could indicate they must consider three options prior to making a recommendation. In practical terms, this means they must present the solution they've already decided they want, and two more—one of which will be yours.

Your coaching can help bring your salespeople in off the ledge and avoid massive wasted time and effort during these *shopping expeditions*. Chances are that your salespeople will be highly motivated to go after the business. You can help them objectively examine the opportunity and then decide whether it is viable, potentially winnable, and worthy of time and effort. Most often, it isn't.

Another common disconnect we see involves an overestimation of the buyers' progress through their buying process. This typically unfolds as the mismatch we see in Figure 8.6. The salesperson thinks the buyer is in the assess solutions stage, when in reality, the buyer hasn't moved past the needs identification stage. This is just the opposite of the situation we've described above. Intuitively, this seems odd. How could this happen?

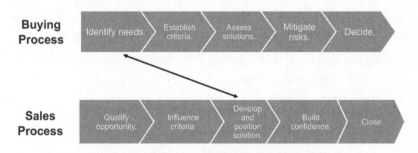

FIGURE 8.6 Mismatch Between the Stage the Buyers Are in and the Stage the Seller Is In

This scenario often unfolds when salespeople have an existing relationship with a customer or prospect, and they are attempting to generate an opportunity. After all, that's the salesperson's job, to generate and win business. The problem arises when the salesperson is persistent (which is good), so the prospect is willing to learn more about the salesperson's solution (which is also good). Once the buyer learns about the salesperson's solution (which is interesting), the buyer may ask for a proposal or quote (which is bad). This is when things get problematic. *Of course* the salesperson is going to give the prospect a proposal or quote. This feels productive to the salesperson. It feels like a buying signal. Oops, not so fast.

In this situation, the buyer has expressed interest because the salesperson has *shown the buyer something interesting*. Not because the buyer has any pressing business need or problem. The buyer probably doesn't have a budget or time frame. The buyer doesn't exhibit any of the characteristics associated with the *assess solutions* stage of the buying process because the buyer is not *in* the assess solutions stage. The buyer is at the *identify needs* stage.

Bloated pipelines are full of these kinds of aspirational opportunities. Ones that are *not really* opportunities yet. They may become opportunities at some point, but they will not do so until the buyer has some reason to move forward. This does not mean salespeople shouldn't pursue these types of situations. It just means that they must do two things more effectively. First, salespeople must accurately identify where the buyer is in the buying process and reflect that in the sales CRM system. Just because the buyer has received a proposal, it doesn't mean that the buyer is at the assess solutions stage. Second, salespeople must get better at building a business case to help move the buyer forward in the buyer's own purchasing process. Until that happens, these opportunities are not real and should not be considered as such.

STRUCTURING OPPORTUNITY COACHING CONVERSATIONS

In Chapter 5, we explored the mechanisms sales managers can use to structure their coaching conversations for maximum impact. We identified the use of agendas to ensure that the coaching covered the right points. We discussed the identification of inputs to ensure proper preparation on the part of the manager and the salesperson. We discussed the need to have specific documented outputs to ensure accountability and execution of specific activities. These elements of structure will differ depending on the type of activity being coached. Because we know that focusing opportunity coaching on the early stages of a deal leads to better performance, we will orient our structuring suggestions accordingly.

Figure 8.7 indicates some of the more common inputs, agenda items, and outputs that drive effective opportunity coaching discussions. These are general guidelines and will need to be adapted for the unique attributes of the opportunities your salespeople pursue.

Inputs	Agenda Items	Outputs
• Existing opportunity plans and/or competitive analysis • Notes from CRM • Pipeline stage criteria	• Establish level of qualification. • Determine viability of fit. • Determine next steps and actions for opportunity pursuit.	• Opportunity strategy • Needed resources • Time frame

FIGURE 8.7 **Common Elements of Effective Opportunity Coaching Discussions**

We have also provided guidance on the importance of collaboration during coaching conversations. Asking good, relevant questions during the coaching discussion will lead to better dialogue, richer insights, and better critical thinking on the part of the salesperson. We offer the following list of questions as a guide to help ensure that the conversations are highly collaborative and relevant. You will most certainly have additional questions you want to ask during your opportunity coaching discussions; however, this list should form a good foundation from which to build.

Early-Stage Opportunity Coaching Questions

- What is your understanding of the company, opportunity, and our solution fit?

- Is the opportunity qualified? Why?

- What are the prospects or customers trying to do? What are their needs and business issues?

- Who are the key decision-makers? How will they buy from you? Where are they in the buying process?

- Why will they buy from us? What is our value proposition, and what is their perception of us (including history)?

- Who is competing for the business? How will we win and why?

- What do you know and not know, and how can you close gaps in your knowledge?

- What are your next steps?

Although we've provided suggested agenda topics for an opportunity coaching discussion, it is also useful to consider how many opportunities you should discuss in any given coaching discussion. Most formally scheduled opportunity coaching conversations involve a discussion of more than one opportunity. But how many is the right amount? How many is too many? In our experience, we've found that two or three opportunities is about the limit of what can realistically be covered in a one-hour coaching conversation. If you attempt to discuss more than that, it is highly likely that your conversations will become superficial, directive, and oriented toward inspection rather than being a rich collaborative coaching dialogue.

Opportunity Plans

In some cases, organizations require salespeople to capture their opportunity strategy in a formal opportunity plan. These plans vary by organization and by complexity of the opportunity stages. The longer and more complex the sales cycle, the more comprehensive the associated opportunity plan and the more likely formal plans are required. A sample opportunity plan is provided for your reference in Figure 8.8.

As you might expect, planning rigor and formality affect performance. A dangerous trend regarding opportunity planning is to overengineer the plans. Not all opportunities salespeople pursue are equally complex enough

Opportunity Qualification and Management Form

Company	
Opportunity	
Team Leader	
Last Update	

Qualification

| Defined Need | | Winnable? | |
| Approved Budget | | Timeline to Purchase | |

Buyers

Name	Type	Needs	Level of Support

Competition

Company	Strengths	

Strategy

Offering	Value Proposition	

Next Steps

Objective	Person Responsible	Action Item / Completion Date

Stage

| Lead | Qualified | Demo | Proposal | Win/Loss |

FIGURE 8.8 **Sales Opportunity Plan**

to warrant a formal plan. One of the first decisions sales managers must make is which opportunities warrant this type of planning.

In our study of management coaching practices, we found that high-performing managers were more likely to require formal plans for only a subset of opportunities versus all opportunities. Lower-performing managers were not as deliberate and were more likely to require formal plans for *all* opportunities. This lack of established criteria for formal plans not only negatively affects performance, but it also impairs salespeople with an unnecessary administrative burden. As usual, formality matters but in limited doses. Moderation is advised.

When opportunity plans are at the right level of complexity, they can form the basis of effective opportunity coaching discussions. Many commercially available opportunity plans come with detailed coaching guides that can provide fodder for coaching conversations at different stages of the sales cycle. Most are not aligned with a buying process; however, they do offer guidance for conducting coaching discussions in the early, mid, and late stages of an opportunity.

FINDING THE RIGHT RHYTHM OF OPPORTUNITY COACHING

The final element of formality needed to operationalize effective opportunity coaching involves selecting the right frequency and duration of opportunity coaching discussions. Once you've determined that opportunity coaching is important, and you've structured your coaching conversations for maximum impact, you must figure out how to conduct these coaching discussions in a repeatable and predictable way.

Managers at all performance levels are more likely to schedule opportunity planning discussions rather than conduct them as needed. However, this trend is higher for high-performing managers. Figure 8.9 illustrates this trend. An interesting twist to this finding is that high-performing managers exhibit even higher levels of coaching formality with salespeople who are below 75 percent of quota. They tend to increase their level of formality when coaching lower-performing salespeople. Although all managers exhibit more formality when coaching lower-performing salespeople, this trend is significantly higher for high-performing managers.

In addition to orienting toward formal scheduling of opportunity coaching discussions, high-performing managers tend to conduct these meetings as scheduled a higher percentage of the time. They *schedule* coaching discussions, and they *conduct* them as scheduled. This means that coaching *intentions* for high performers are more likely to lead to coaching *behaviors*. Because this tendency to develop an opportunity coaching rhythm and stick to it is correlated to higher performance, it warrants a deeper examination.

What are the nuances that allow high performers to successfully establish and execute rhythms that work? That's the secret sauce of high-performing

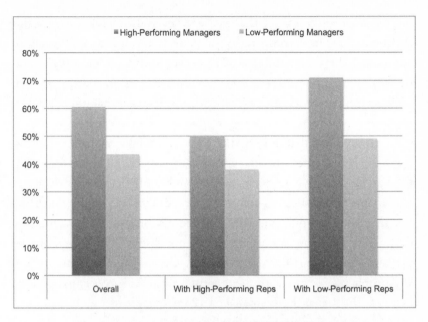

FIGURE 8.9 **Percent of Managers Who Schedule
Opportunity Planning Meetings**

managers, and there's more than one recipe. Although we can't give you an exact formula for the opportunity coaching rhythm you should choose for your sales team, we can give you very helpful *patterns* exhibited by high-performing managers. You can use these patterns as guidelines in developing your own coaching rhythm.

The first consideration is the *length of a typical sales cycle*. In our research, we found that the longer the sales cycles, the less frequently managers conducted opportunity coaching discussions. This ties back to our earlier point about the minimum level of rigor needed to get the job done. If conducting monthly opportunity coaching discussions with each of your salespeople is effective, then don't attempt to do this every two weeks. The frequency must reflect an adequate amount of time to allow change in the buying process.

High-performing managers tend to meet *less frequently* than low-performing managers for their opportunity coaching discussions. This trend is significant. The most common frequency for high-performing managers was monthly opportunity coaching discussions. Lower-performing managers tended to meet either weekly or every two weeks. The specific rhythm differed from company to company; however, the trend remained consistent. This does not mean that *you* should conduct monthly opportunity coaching discussions. There are other factors, in addition to sales cycle length, that must be taken into consideration that affect a viable rhythm.

One factor in determining the right coaching rhythm is the *size of your team*. A manager who manages 6 salespeople has a lot more flexibility than a manager who manages 10. You literally have to *do the math*. How many hours of opportunity coaching can you realistically incorporate into your schedule and still have the flexibility to address needs as they arise? Only you can decide. Recall our discussion of our two sales managers within our Fortune 50 client. The manager who managed 4 salespeople people met with them constantly and in a very unstructured manner. The manager who managed 12 salespeople met with each salesperson monthly, in a very structured rhythm.

As usual, we advise a *less-is-better* approach. If you are meeting monthly and it is insufficient, you can always increase your frequency. It is not as easy to start with a higher frequency and back off. All too often, managers who design their rhythms aggressively are in a constant state of canceling and rescheduling their coaching discussions. The problem is that overaggressive rhythms work only under optimal conditions, which do not exist in a sales force. On the surface, it may seem counterintuitive to set the bar low, to meet less often versus more often; however, this is what high performers do. And it works.

We are not suggesting that less coaching is better than more coaching. What we are saying is that there is not a direct positive correlation between time spent coaching and high performance. In our research we found a positive correlation between a *moderate* amount of coaching and high performance. High-performing managers conduct a moderate amount of coaching, and they do it *differently* than their lower-performing peers do. High performers are more *consistent* and *predictable* in the way they interact with the salespeople they manage. They realize that coaching time is precious, and they make the most of it.

Once you determine the appropriate format and realistic frequency for your opportunity coaching discussions, you must land on a *duration* for each meeting. This is the area where a less-is-better approach is not as effective. What do we mean? Well, high-performing managers may meet less often than their lower-performing peers; however, the discussions they have are richer and of a longer duration. They tend to spend an hour conducting their opportunity coaching discussions, whereas lower-performing managers tend to spend 30 minutes or less. Fewer, but richer coaching opportunity conversations is the key to getting more of your salespeople to quota.

Case Study: Putting It All Together

We return to our Fortune 50 client for a real-case scenario of opportunity coaching. This client had a serious business problem. They had a target of 20 percent growth in revenue over a five-year period. This was a daunting growth target, particularly for a mature business. They could not figure out how to achieve this target with the existing business conditions. Something had to change.

This client's performance was flat, their sales forecasts were erratic, and their win rates were low. This same client had invested heavily in tools, technology, and training for their salespeople and their sales managers. They didn't know what to do to turn things around. They felt they had tried everything and nothing was working. They were incredibly smart people and very capable. They just didn't know which lever to pull to get them headed in the right direction.

We pulled their leadership team together to determine which levers were most likely to result in revenue growth. We used the results-objectives-activities framework to identify target activities for coaching. The output of this discussion is reflected in Figure 8.10.

It seemed that the culprit in most of their ills was in the health of their pipeline. Lots of bad deals were bouncing around in their pipeline consuming resources and not resulting in wins. The only way for this client to get on a better path was to pay more attention to deals before those deals

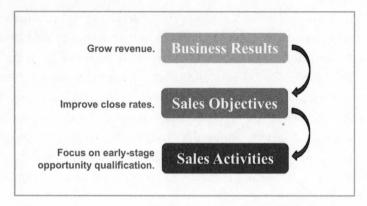

FIGURE 8.10 **Identify the Coachable *Activities***

got into the pipeline. Once deals were in the pipeline, they got lots of attention and resources. They just needed to ensure that those resources were spent on winnable deals.

If salespeople needed to do a better job of qualifying deals, then the managers' coaching effort would have to focus on this critical activity. They needed to formalize early-stage deal coaching to accomplish the task of cleaning up their pipelines and improving their win rates. It was a bit scary for a company that had flat performance to engage in behaviors that could potentially shrink their pipeline, but initially that was what they needed to do.

We then set about the process of helping them structure these early-stage coaching conversations. Recall from Chapter 5 that good coaching conversations incorporate inputs, outputs, and agendas. Their inputs, outputs, and agendas needed to be specific and focus on early-stage opportunity qualification. The inputs and outputs they identified are reflected in Figure 8.11. The inputs were highly specific to ensure the appropriate level of preparation for both sales managers and salespeople to enable rich discussion. Salespeople were required to update their CRM system prior to the coaching meeting, come prepared to discuss progress on current opportunities, and provide updates on action items from previous coaching discussions. Outputs included agreed-upon actions from the current coaching discussion and follow-up items for the sales managers.

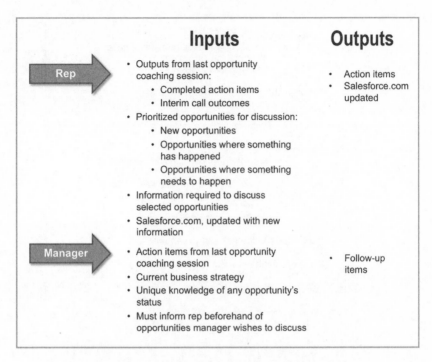

FIGURE 8.11 Inputs and Outputs for Coaching Conversations

An agenda was developed to ensure that coaching discussions unfolded in predictable ways and got to the desired level of detail. The goal was to have rich dialogue on a few early-stage opportunities. The tendency was for managers to have superficial conversations about many late-stage opportunities, which was clearly not having the desired effect on close rates and associated revenue growth. Sales managers needed very specific guidance on what to do and how to do it. They needed to be very clear on how this new approach was different from what they were used to doing. Figure 8.12 is the core agenda managers used for the early-stage coaching discussions.

The details of the agenda ensured that the most critical topics regarding each opportunity would be discussed. Managers didn't have to figure this out and come up with a solution on their own. If you examine the items on this agenda, you will notice that the items were posed as questions. This was by design. The goal was to create rich, collaborative coaching dialogue. Questions drive higher levels of collaboration. You will

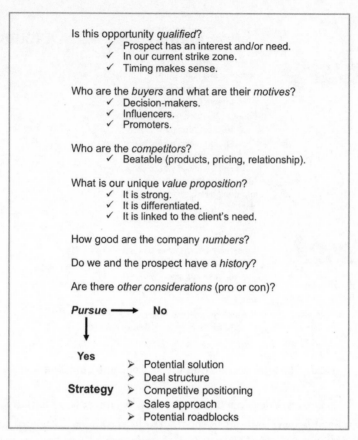

Is this opportunity *qualified*?
    ✓ Prospect has an interest and/or need.
    ✓ In our current strike zone.
    ✓ Timing makes sense.

Who are the *buyers* and what are their *motives*?
    ✓ Decision-makers.
    ✓ Influencers.
    ✓ Promoters.

Who are the *competitors*?
    ✓ Beatable (products, pricing, relationship).

What is our unique *value proposition*?
    ✓ It is strong.
    ✓ It is differentiated.
    ✓ It is linked to the client's need.

How good are the company *numbers*?

Do we and the prospect have a *history*?

Are there *other considerations* (pro or con)?

Pursue ⟶ **No**

⬇

Yes
    ➤ Potential solution
    ➤ Deal structure
Strategy ➤ Competitive positioning
    ➤ Sales approach
    ➤ Potential roadblocks

FIGURE 8.12 Core Agenda Used for Early-Stage Coaching Discussions for Deals in Lead, Opportunity Identification, and Proposal Stages

also notice that the agenda was not overly packed with items. Fewer topics, covered in greater depth was the goal. Fewer topics, fewer opportunities, covered in greater detail. Moderation in the *number* of topics, but not in the *depth* of topics.

To ensure that the sales managers got to the desired level of depth, an additional tool was developed. We helped this client develop a simple, yet comprehensive coaching guide for these early-stage coaching conversations. The guide addressed only the first three stages of their sales process because those were considered early stage. The first three stages of their sales process also lacked clarity and were not consistently addressed across the management team.

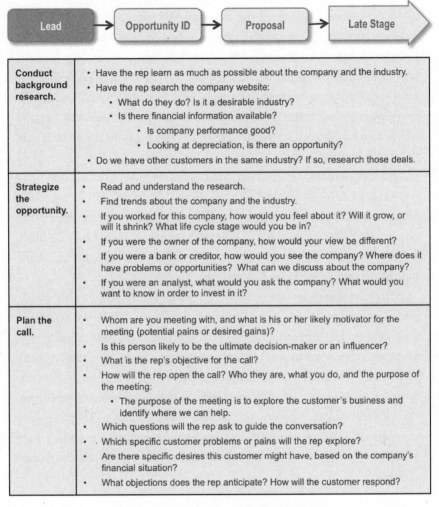

FIGURE 8.13 **Early-Stage Coaching Guide**

Figure 8.13 reflects the first of a three-page coaching guide. The detail for each stage included the types of research salespeople needed to conduct, suggestions for how to strategize the opportunity at each stage, and tips for helping salespeople plan upcoming sales calls during this stage. Managers had this tool as a reference to help them achieve the level of desired depth in each coaching conversation. The structure of inputs, outputs, agenda, and coaching guide left nothing to chance. Before we worked with them, managers were not crystal clear on what constituted an early-stage coaching conversation.

So, now we've examined the selection of a coachable activity (early-stage opportunity qualification), tied directly to the desired sales objective (improved win rates), enabling the overall desired business result of increased revenue. We explored the structure this client put in place for their early-stage coaching conversations via inputs, outputs, agenda, and coaching guide. Recall from prior chapters that operationalizing desired coaching into the sales managers' day-to-day job is a critical step to ensure that coaching happens.

In the case of this client's sales managers, they were already conducting weekly one-on-one pipeline reviews with each of their salespeople. They had a culture of formality already in place, only the formality was not oriented toward the right topics. These sales managers were busy. Their average reporting ratio was nine salespeople per manager. That's nine hours per week of pipeline reviews.

The managers were not receptive to putting more things on their already busy schedules, so we had to make a trade-off. When we examined their sales cycles, it became clear that deal progression didn't change significantly from week to week. The pipeline reviews did not need to happen weekly. The managers could gain valuable coaching time by limiting the pipeline reviews to every other week. This allowed them to repurpose two of the four coaching sessions to early-stage coaching. They kept the same overall number of scheduled coaching hours and repurposed half of them. Figure 8.14 shows the adjusted rhythm of their coaching conversations.

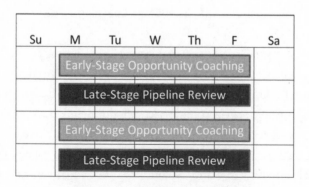

FIGURE 8.14 **Management Rhythm**

This effort was extremely targeted and comprehensive. We worked with this client to isolate the types of things that salespeople and sales managers needed to be doing, and doing consistently to achieve their revenue targets. We helped them do the heavy lifting of putting together a plan that would lead to the right type and quantity of coaching. We would love to say that this unfolded without incident and that all sales managers actively embraced the new approach. That didn't happen.

What did happen, and almost always happens in real organizations attempting real change, was that some managers willingly embraced change and others resisted. Some managers lean in to the change and execute heartily, while others go through the motions. This situation was no different. As comprehensive as we were with this client, there was another level of detail that was required. The sales director, who managed the sales managers, had to be involved—and he was.

Sales managers needed to be held accountable for conducting the coaching sessions effectively and using the tools provided. The sales director had his own rhythm of coaching observation. He saw firsthand the degree to which managers were effectively coaching early-stage opportunities. And he was only mildly pleased. About half of the sales managers were actively embracing the new approach to coaching. The other half were either just going through the motions or ignoring the approach altogether. Here's the interesting thing: if the sales director had not periodically observed these coaching sessions, he wouldn't have known the degree to which the organization's efforts were being sabotaged.

Through a process of observation and feedback, the sale director was able to get all of his managers on track over time. Those who were executing well were acknowledged and their efforts reinforced. Those who were not were guided toward the right behaviors. This didn't happen overnight. It took about four months for the sales director to feel confident that the coaching was happening consistently across the sales management team.

This experience was an epiphany for the sales director. Prior to this initiative, he had never listened in on any coaching conversations between his sales managers and salespeople. He was amazed at the variation that existed at the outset of this engagement. By about the four-month point, he was seeing consistency in the way his salespeople were being coached.

He was also able to glean best practices of individual managers and parlay those across the management team. He shared that he never realized how little he knew about how his managers were coaching and managing their teams. He was a new man. Armed and dangerous. And effective.

The telltale signs of effective activity coaching are better outcomes. In our parlance, we are looking for consistent execution of key sales activities, to drive positive movement in sales objectives (leading indicators) to ultimately get to the business results we want. In this client's case, their sales objective was improved close rates. You can see their results in Figure 8.15. They had significant improvement in both deal win rates and forecasted revenue won. We tracked this trend over an 18-month period to ensure that their progress was sustained.

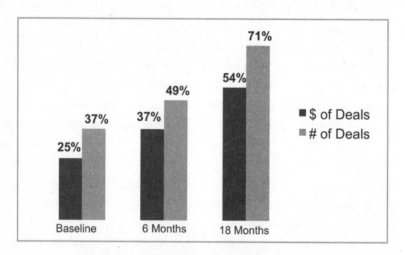

FIGURE 8.15 **Our Client's Meaningfully Improved Deal Win Rates and Forecasted Revenue Won**

The right needles were moving, in the right directions, sustained over time. This was an incredibly successful change initiative. Deal win rates nearly doubled during the indicated time frame, and the percentage of forecasted revenue won more than doubled during the same period. This was a fantastic outcome, and it reinforced the power of small changes to coaching practices leading to big outcomes. The good news did not stop there. This client had done a survey of their salespeople prior to our engagement, and they were dismayed by the dearth of coaching that was happening. They redeployed the survey six months after the launch of the engagement, and they saw a big rise the amount of coaching their salespeople reported receiving. Figure 8.16 shows the amount of coaching salespeople reported receiving before and after the adjusted coaching practices.

Coaching Received per Salesperson per Month	Prior to Training	6 Months Post-Training	Change
<3 hours	48%	9%	−39%
3–5 hours	35%	62%	+27%
>5 hours	17%	29%	+12%

FIGURE 8.16 Increases in the Perceived Volume of Coaching

The fascinating thing about this outcome was that the managers were spending exactly the same number of hours each week coaching each salesperson. All they did was change the *type* of coaching they provided. Before the adjustment to their managers' coaching practices, almost half of the salespeople reported receiving less than three hours of coaching per month. After the adjustment was made, over 90 percent of salespeople reported receiving three or more hours of coaching per month. Amazing, but true. This reinforces our point that it is not necessarily the amount of coaching that leads to better performance. It is the type of coaching that is consistently provided that matters.

The reason this story is so powerful and relevant to sales management today is that sales managers have very little discretionary time. The choices they make about coaching—the type and frequency—matter. These managers made a few important changes, without adding any more work to their already overfull plate, and achieved breakthrough results. These are not isolated results. We see these kinds of outcomes in many of our client organizations when they incorporate the types of coaching practices included in this book.

KEY TAKEAWAYS:
OPPORTUNITY COACHING

- The goal of opportunity coaching is to help salespeople qualify, pursue, and win individual deals.

- The more complex the solution and associated buying process, the less likely salespeople are to make quota. Adjusting opportunity coaching to the stage of the customer's buying process helps reduce the negative effect of buying complexity on quota attainment.

- Opportunity coaching is markedly different in the early stages versus the late stages of the buying process. The most successful sales managers are significantly more likely to orient their opportunity coaching effort to the early stages of the buying process.

- The most successful sales managers require opportunity plans but for only a subset of sales opportunities. Less successful managers require plans for all opportunities.

- All sales managers are more likely to formally schedule opportunity coaching discussions, but this trend is higher for high-performing sales managers.

- Successful sales managers conduct a moderate amount of opportunity coaching by conducting fewer coaching discussions of longer duration. High performers conduct opportunity coaching discussions monthly for one hour. Lower-performing managers meet more frequently and for shorter durations.

- High-performing sales managers arrange their schedules to accommodate opportunity coaching discussion by alternating time of day and alternating weeks, providing breaks in between coaching sessions to attend to business demands.

CHAPTER 9

CALL COACHING

Sales calls are the lifeblood, the beating heart, of sales execution. The rest of the body can be relatively healthy, but the heart is where the action lies. If the heart fails, everything else in the body quickly follows suit. Call coaching is the mechanism that keeps the heartbeat of sales strong and steady. Just like the heart, sales calls need monitoring and attention. Ignore them at your own peril.

To make the case for the importance of call coaching, we will go so far as to say that call coaching is to sales what calling plays is to sports. No matter how great the play, it must be executed well to work. The same applies to sales. No matter how brilliant the sales strategy, the success or failure of that strategy rides on the *quality* of the *individual interactions* your salespeople execute. One bad sales call can torpedo the chances of winning a deal. Like it or not, call coaching is vital to helping your salespeople succeed.

In this chapter, we will examine the various ways sales managers provide call coaching to the salespeople they manage. We will explore call coaching via call planning, call observation, and feedback of observed calls as the various ways call coaching can occur. As usual, we will reveal coaching practices of high-performing managers and contrast them with practices of lower-performing managers.

It is probably not surprising that the highest-performing sales managers take call coaching very seriously. The most successful sales managers in our study, the ones that have 75 percent or more of their salespeople at quota, are more likely than their lower-performing peers to *formally request* time to help their salespeople plan upcoming calls. Figure 9.1 shows that 15 percent more high performers request coaching discussions compared with lower performers. High-performing managers don't leave this to chance. They *proactively* identify important sales calls and *request* time to help coach their salespeople to prepare for those calls.

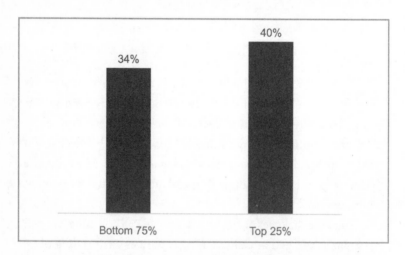

FIGURE 9.1 **Managers Proactively Request Coaching Discussions**

Another interesting trend illustrated in Figure 9.2 has to do with the tendency to coach because the managers are attending the sales call. Our research revealed that a larger percentage of low-performing managers *primarily* help their salespeople plan sales calls because they are *attending* the sales calls. We agree that helping salespeople plan sales calls the managers are attending is a good thing. It makes perfect sense. It would be silly not to plan calls you are attending. But that shouldn't be the primary reason you plan sales calls with your salespeople, and that is not the case with high performers.

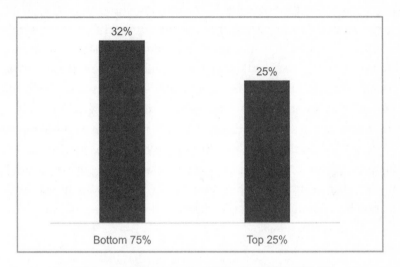

FIGURE 9.2 **Managers Coach the Calls They Attend**

When you look at the trend of high performers versus lower performers, the number one reason high performers help their salespeople plan a sales call is because of the *importance of the sales call*. Over 40 percent of high-performing managers reported that they plan calls because they proactively request the planning discussion. Only 25 percent of high performers reported that they primarily help salespeople plan calls they are attending. High performers are strongly oriented to proactive call planning *regardless* of whether they attend those calls. High performers know that thorough preparation and planning lead to better call execution. Period.

COACHING SALES CALLS
ACROSS THE BUYING PROCESS

So, how do high performers help set up their salespeople for highly effective sales interactions? Well, when high-performing managers coach their salespeople to better execute individual sales calls, they adjust their call coaching efforts in much the same way that they adjust their opportunity coaching efforts: they align their efforts according to the stage of the customers' buying process. This additional filter of buying process stage helps ensure that their coaching efforts are most effective.

Buyers' interests change as an opportunity progresses, and so must the salesperson's approach to individual interactions within that opportunity. Although all sales conversations will have similar elements, the actual *content* of the conversations varies widely at different points along the buying process. Unfortunately, most call coaching methodologies don't address this important distinction. Figure 9.3 is an example of a typical buying process. We did a thorough introduction of typical sales activities, coaching practices, and coaching errors for each stage of the buying process in the last chapter on opportunity coaching. We will not repeat that information here, but instead we will expand on the call execution elements of each buying process stage.

FIGURE 9.3 **Buyers' Goals at Various Stages in the Buying Process**

Identify Needs

Coaching for sales calls that are in the *identify needs stage* of the buying process is oriented toward helping salespeople understand and shape buyer needs, tease out the details of the decision-making process, and qualify the opportunity. Proper planning for these early-stage calls ensures that sellers are well prepared to dig into the details of the clients' environment, understand the size and scope of the problems that exist, and build out those problems to drive client urgency. No urgency, no action.

The first order of business is *understanding buyer needs*. Salespeople need to find out why the buyers are considering making a change. What are they hoping to be able to do that they can't do now? What issues are they hoping to resolve? Call coaching must help salespeople uncover details about buyer problems and desires and help salespeople ask good, probing questions to get buyers to articulate what is happening in their current environment. It is also vital to ensure that your salespeople understand the needs and issues of *each* buyer. Most complex deals involve multiple buyers with varying needs.

Good call coaching helps equip salespeople to question their buyers about the *cost of inaction*—what happens if the buyer does nothing. It is getting more and more important for salespeople to be prepared to monetize buyer problems and quantify the cost of inaction. This is particularly important because it will help the salesperson quantify return on investment in conversations later in the buying process.

It is also important to ensure that your salespeople truly understand the *process the buyer will use to make the decision*. Good call coaching can ensure that your salespeople understand the different players involved, their relative influence on the buying decision, the timeline required, and how these types of decisions have been made in the past. Salespeople often assume that the person they're dealing with is the one making the decision—which is rarely the case.

Call coaching at the identify needs stage is designed to ensure that salespeople properly *qualify opportunities and ensure that they are worthy of pursuit*. Thorough understanding and evidence of buyer needs, decision-makers, and the decision-making process, timelines, and cost of inaction are vital to proper qualification. The most effective sales managers coach to this level of detail and require evidence that these types of conversations unfold between their salespeople and their prospective buyers.

A special, yet frequent situation in this stage is when buyers are proactive about solving a problem, but they are looking to solve the wrong problem. The buyers appear to be closer along in their buying process, but upon further examination, they have not truly fleshed out the right problem. In our business, as in many businesses, we get a fair amount of inbound leads. Buyers will reach out to us if they have a problem we can solve. It is very important to ensure that we truly understand the issues they are facing, because different solutions solve different problems.

EXAMPLE

Coaching Conversation to Help the Salesperson Identify the Buyers' Needs

One of our salespeople received an inbound lead from our website requesting information on our sales forecasting program. The salesperson had a brief initial call with the buyer who shared that her company's forecasts were inaccurate. It was a problem, and her company wanted to train the managers on forecasting techniques to improve the quality and accuracy of their forecasts.

Our sales manager had seen this situation before, and the following call coaching conversation unfolded:

Sales manager: Tell me, when you asked about the reasons the managers' forecasts were inaccurate, what did you learn?

Salesperson: Well, they said that they are now tracking forecast accuracy as one of their key metrics, and they are pretty far off every month.

Sales manager: Yes, I understand. Did the buyers say why the forecasts were inaccurate? How are the forecasts created? Is it the method they use to forecast, or is it the data that is the problem?

Salesperson: I'm not sure. What do you mean by a problem with the data?

Coach: When I've encountered this situation before, the inaccurate forecasts are a symptom of poor pipeline management. If salespeople don't put the opportunities into the CRM correctly, with the right revenue amount and the appropriate sales cycle stage, the forecast that is created cannot be trusted. Whether or not the prospect has the right forecasting methodology, they can't create a viable forecast with bad information.

Salesperson: I see. That makes sense. I can see that I need to do some more digging to better understand what the real problem is before I sell them the wrong thing.

Sales manager: Yes. So, how will you position this next call with the buyers so that they are willing to consider that they might have a different problem than forecasting?

Salesperson: I'll explain that oftentimes when buyers think they have a forecasting problem, it's really something else that is showing up as a forecasting problem.

Sales manager: You might need to explain that a bit more. If I were the buyers, that wouldn't quite convince me. How could you expand on that to set up a bit more context?

Salesperson: I'll tell her that I need to better understand what is causing the forecasting problem so that I can recommend the right solution— one that will get at the root causes of the problem. We may find out that it is forecasting, or it might be something else. Either way, we can help them.

Sales manager: Good. It's tough to move buyers off a particular solution if they think it is the right one. You have to earn the right to back them up in their own buying process—which is sometimes hard to do. What you just said will help accomplish that. Now, what questions will you ask to ensure that you understand the underlying issues?

Salesperson: I will ask about her perceptions of CRM compliance. To what degree is she confident that the salespeople are inputting accurate deal information, including the revenue projections, sales cycle stage, and projected close date.

Sales manager: Good. What else?

Salesperson: I will explore the method they use to create the forecast to determine if the method is affected by inaccurate data. I will also ask about the health of their pipelines and whether they have a method for determining whether salespeople are putting deals in accurately, by stage.

Sales manager: That sounds right. If we can get at the underlying details of how deals are captured, including the compliance of data input, we can determine whether this is a pipeline problem or a forecasting problem.

Salesperson: Agreed. Thanks. That was helpful. I'll let you know what happens.

Sales manager: Perfect. Let me know if there is anything else I can do to help.

DEBRIEF

As you might suspect, our salesperson did a thorough job on the next sales call with the buyer and helped the buyer realize that it was not a forecasting problem at all. CRM compliance was low, salespeople were waiting until the last minute to put deals into the system, and the information regarding each opportunity was suspect. Until they solved the pipeline management problem, they were never going to solve the forecasting problem. We steered them away from our forecasting program to our pipeline coaching program. It was a much better fit. This helped build buyer confidence in their solution choice, and it also cemented our credibility as experts in understanding and remedying the pipeline and forecasting issues.

Why is it so important to dig into the details of buyer problems at the identify needs stage? Why such an intentional focus on understanding the true size and scope of buyer problems? Because people are twice as likely to take action to *avoid pain* as they are to *achieve gain*. Renowned behavioral economist Daniel Kahneman identified this tendency and coined the term *loss aversion*. How something is framed matters. Frame it as a loss and people take action. For example, people would rather avoid a $5 surcharge than get a $5 discount.

Pain must be real, quantified, and urgent for change to happen. This is the primary reason why call coaching in the identify needs stage is so important and powerful. If you can get your salespeople prepared to dig into the thorny details of client problems, they will be far more effective at building urgency and developing real opportunities—ones that end up in a win versus a stalled deal.

> **People are twice as likely to take action to avoid pain than to achieve gain.**

There is so much noise in the marketplace about the buyers being almost to the end of their buying process before they engage with salespeople. Although it is true that buyers do more research than they used to and they are more educated than ever on your solutions, they don't necessarily reach conclusions that are in the best interest of their buying decision. In truth, buyers often *think* they are further along than they are. And this is a dangerous trend. It is in just these sorts of situations that the best salespeople become value-added consultants rather than order takers. This is where call coaching can prepare your salespeople to differentiate based on how they sell and not just what they sell.

Establish Criteria

Coaching for sales calls in the *establish criteria stage* of the buying process prepares sellers to understand and shape buying criteria, determine the competitive landscape, and set themselves up for effective competitive differentiation. These elements are important in helping salespeople shape deals in a way that sets them up to win. Salespeople who excel in this stage of the buying process make it easier for buyers to buy, maximize the perceived value of their solutions, and minimize the likelihood of competitive threats.

The first order of business is coaching your salespeople to quantify needs into tangible buying criteria. Salespeople need a strategy to accomplish this task. This is a rich coaching opportunity because buying criteria become the measuring stick for how buyers will evaluate solutions. Which needs should the salesperson focus on for this purpose? Well, the ones that are relevant to the buyers and provide the best opportunity for competitive differentiation. This means that your salespeople have to know which needs are important to the buyers and which alternatives the buyers are considering.

For example, your salesperson may have uncovered several needs that must be addressed. The salesperson may have also found out that the buyers are considering competitors A and B. The most effective coaching will help the salesperson identify which needs are most important to the buyers, as well as which needs are *better met by your salesperson's solutions*. You can then focus your call coaching efforts to help your salesperson shape those needs and quantify them into criteria that will best position your solutions.

EXAMPLE

Coaching Conversation to Help Salesperson Work with Buyer to Establish Buying Criteria

Let me provide an example from my time at Xerox Corporation. When I (Michelle) was a salesperson for Xerox, I sold copiers. Lots of them. At that time, Xerox copiers cost at least twice as much our competitors' products. It also didn't help that our competitors' copiers had more than twice as many features as ours. So I sold the most expensive copiers with the fewest features.

As you might imagine, this was not an easy task. Getting my customers to pay significantly more for a machine that offered fewer features required a very deliberate sales approach. I had to uncover needs and qualify in a way that quickly established my solution dominance. The following example illustrates how my excellent sales manager, Trevor, coached me to shape needs into buying criteria that matched my solution strengths:

Trevor: Michelle, I realize that our copiers are more expensive, but we have some very clear strengths that we can leverage when selling to law firms. What is the number one need that you've uncovered with this legal administrator?

Michelle: High quality. She was very adamant about wanting high quality.

Trevor: OK, that's good, but all vendors are going to say that they have high quality. What is it about our quality that is superior to the competition?

Michelle: Well, everyone's quality looks good when you're only making a few copies, but ours maintains quality over long runs. The competitors' quality degrades, and there are significant quality declines after about 50 pages or so.

Trevor: OK, is this law firm running large jobs? Do many of their documents exceed 50 pages?

Michelle: Yes, they have plenty of jobs that are 100 pages or longer. They copy very large contracts, briefs, and other documents.

Trevor: So, when the legal administrator says that quality is important, how can you clarify that need in a way that plays to our strengths?

Michelle: I could confirm that she has many large copy jobs that exceed 100 pages in length. Then I could ask her how important it is to maintain quality, even during these large jobs.

Trevor: Good, I think that would work. What if she says yes? What else can you ask to cement the importance of consistent quality on long runs?

Michelle: I could ask a clarifying question like, "So, are you saying that the way you define quality is that the copier maintains consistently high quality, even on very long runs?"

Trevor: Yes, it needs to be her idea, not yours. If you can get her to agree on this more specific definition of quality, could you plant some doubt about the other machines she is considering?

Michelle: Well, I could ask her if she would consider a machine a poor fit for her firm if it could not maintain consistent quality on the types of jobs she was running.

Trevor: Yes, that would certainly make her question the viability of some of the vendors she is considering.

DEBRIEF

In this situation, Trevor asked me to first identify what was important to the buyers. He wanted to know what needs had to be met. Armed with this information, he was able to shape my knowledge of our competitive strengths into powerful questions I could ask to shape the way these buyers thought about quality. He didn't stop once he knew I understood our differentiator. He probed until I had shown evidence that I could *ask questions* to influence the way the buyers perceived the differentiator. This is the heart of call coaching. As a coach, Trevor probed until he had solid evidence that I could navigate the conversation with the buyers. He took me beyond just understanding buyer needs, and coached me to shape those needs into quantified buying criteria.

Fast-forward to the end of the story. I won the deal. I won many deals in much the same way. I had a sales manager who was an excellent sales coach. He and I spent many hours hashing through the specifics of these types of conversations. He dug into the details with me until I was armed and dangerous. As a coach, your efforts at helping salespeople think through the specific behaviors needed to accomplish this important task will dramatically improve their ability to compete—compete in ways that increase their chances of winning more deals.

Assess Solutions

Once buyers have a clear idea of what they want, and hopefully a set of defined buying criteria, they go about the task of evaluating potential providers. They want to find out which provider is the right fit for them so they can make the best choice. It is in this *assess solutions stage* that the solutions are scoped, proposals are provided, demonstrations are conducted, and every salesperson tries to position *their* solution as the best one. Coaching to this stage is vital to increase the chances of becoming a finalist and ultimately winning a deal.

The better the job the salesperson has done developing and shaping buying criteria, the smoother this stage will go. What gets tricky is that buying criteria often change in this stage. New buying criteria can emerge, shifting the relative importance of prior criteria. Sales calls conducted in this stage involve proposal presentations, demonstrations, trial runs, and other types of activities involved in demonstrating the fit between the sellers' solutions and the buyers' needs.

An important goal of call coaching in this stage is to ensure that salespeople understand the competitive landscape. Sellers who are most effective find out with whom they are competing, the solutions their competitors are providing, and the buyers' perception of each solution. It is shocking to me how many salespeople give this short shrift. Even very experienced salespeople. We honestly don't know how salespeople can effectively position their offering if they don't thoroughly understand the range of solutions the buyers are considering. Learning which solutions buyers are evaluating speaks volumes about the buyers' thought process. It also helps salespeople prepare offensive and defensive strategies to better position their solution against those of their competitors.

Call coaching prior to a solution presentation is primarily geared toward ensuring that the salesperson has clarified the criteria buyers will use to make their decision and that the salesperson has gained information about competitors under consideration. Call coaching at this stage is designed to help salespeople present their offering in a way that is highly relevant, compelling, and differentiated from other solutions being considered. Several aspects of planning should be considered, including content of presentation, relevant examples, and mitigation strategies where the sellers' solution may be weak.

When coaching for sales calls in this stage, sales managers can ensure that salespeople have the right kind of information relating to buyer needs and criteria, sufficient examples and proof sources to lend credibility, and a plan for engaging each buyer during the presentation. Different buyers will have different buying criteria. As a coach, you can help your salespeople think through the criteria of these different buyers and how to best respond to each during the solution presentation.

In addition to helping salespeople develop their presentations, it is quite valuable to have them do a trial run. It is remarkable what we can learn, as coaches, when we see how the plan unfolds in a live conversation. We may find that the salespeople forget to ask questions. We may find that the examples or stories they included didn't hit the mark. Alternatively, we may find that the flow was excellent, and not much adjustment is needed. Conducting a trial run becomes increasingly important as deal size increases. The stakes are high, and high stakes warrant thorough preparation.

A special challenge at the assess solutions stage arises when the process the buyers are using to evaluate solutions is not well aligned with the best outcome. This means that effective selling involves adjusting the buyers' evaluation process. This can be quite tricky. Buyers, like all of us humans, like to do things the same way over and over again. We are creatures of habit, and habits are hard to change. Even when they don't serve us well.

EXAMPLE

Coaching Conversation to Help Salesperson Work with Buyer to Assess Solutions

This real example involves a colleague of mine who sold blood analyzers for a medical diagnostic company. Although I (Michelle) wasn't his sales manager, I was in a position to help him, and call coaching was what he needed. I had witnessed him experience similar bad outcomes many times and thought a little call coaching was necessary.

My colleague was expressing frustration that many of his side-by-side evaluations were ending in lost sales. Each of these side-by-side evaluations took several days of his time and many hours of coordination, and they came at great cost to his company. Most prospects would line up three competing blood analyzers for these multiday trials. It was quite an event. At the time of our conversation, my colleague had just lost his fifth deal involving these side-by-side evaluations. Below is an excerpt from our call coaching conversation:

Michelle: Steve, I'm curious why you offer your clients these side-by-side evaluations if they are not helping you win deals.

Steve: Well, this is the way hospital laboratories buy blood analyzers. It has been this way for the 20 years I've been selling them.

Michelle: Yes, I understand why the lab manager would want the side-by-side evaluation. It seems logical that if they see the analyzers together, in their lab, they can easily compare them.

Steve: Yeah, that's why they like to do the evaluations in this manner. I really don't know what to do about it.

Michelle: Do you feel that this side-by-side evaluation is the best way for your buyers to see the real value of the different analyzers?

Steve: No, I don't. It is more of a dog and pony show than anything else.

Michelle: What do you mean?

Steve: Well, the lab staff doesn't really use the analyzers the same way during the trial as they would on a day-to-day basis once they own the equipment. It's not realistic or representative of what they will experience in their lab.

Michelle: Hmmm. Well, if the side-by-side evaluation is not the best way to evaluate the analyzers, what is? What process could your buyers use that would be more effective?

Steve: When I've taken buyers to other labs who are using the equipment and they talk to the lab personnel about what it's like to use our analyzers, it is much more helpful and realistic.

Michelle: So, you've done this before—used reference sites to help your buyers evaluate your analyzers?

Steve: Yes, a few times. It's just not as common.

Michelle: Why?

Steve: Because everyone wants to do the side-by-side.

Michelle: I know you are getting ready to present your proposal, and I'm sure if you don't change the rules, you will find yourself in another side-by-side evaluation. Steve, let's talk about your upcoming sales call. What could you do during your conversation to change the way this lab manager goes about the task of evaluating the various analyzers?

Steve: I don't know.

Michelle: Could you just tell the lab manager that you don't recommend doing a side-by-side evaluation?

Steve: I guess. But that seems risky.

Michelle: Well, you've lost the last five deals. Is there a risk you might lose this one too if you can't change the way the analyzers are evaluated?

Steve: Yes. I guess I could tell him that I don't feel that a side-by-side is the best approach.

Michelle: Well, it matters more what he thinks will be the best approach. Why is it in his best interest to talk to existing customers and visit their labs versus just bringing the analyzers in-house? Walk me through that logic.

Steve: Because these other labs are highly functioning and can give him insight on how the analyzer will operate in their real environment. It is much more meaningful and insightful.

Michelle: Excellent. Can you ask the lab manager whether he is open to considering a more effective way to evaluate the different options?

Steve: Yes. I could tell him that I don't feel that the side-by-side is in his best interest and that I've had other customers benefit from visiting other labs.

Michelle: What if he pushes back and says he wants the side-by-side?

Steve: I can tell him that if he is still unsure after visiting a client site, we can consider the side-by-side. We can use it as a fallback position. I can explain that it will take far less of his staff's time, involve fewer logistical hassles, and give him a more accurate picture of the way the analyzer will work in his lab. Make it a win-win, with the fallback of doing the side-by-side if necessary.

Michelle: Excellent. It sounds like you have a solid plan.

DEBRIEF

In this situation, I had to get Steve to think through, and talk through, viable ways to get the lab manager to consider taking a different approach. The key was to find a way to make it more beneficial to the lab manager to change, rather than beneficial for the salesperson. This was where the finesse came into play. This call coaching conversation was very detailed, but it had to be. Steve had to be ready to navigate the actual conversation with the lab manager. Steve had to be able to turn his idea into an effective conversation. Our call coaching conversation had to get to a level of detail that equipped Steve to execute the sales call in the desired direction.

After several conversations, Steve was able to convince the lab manager that the alternative evaluation method was superior and, indeed, in his lab's best interests. The other solution providers were caught unaware and had to scramble to come up with customer sites that this prospect could visit. Steve had changed the trajectory of this entire opportunity by making just one great, high-impact sales call. He set the rules for how products would be evaluated, and this put him in the best competitive position. He won the deal, and it was one of the largest deals his company had ever won. All because he was willing to change the playing field. He changed his approach to a few key sales calls at this vital stage of the buying process. Call coaching scores again!

Mitigate Risks

Call coaching in this late *mitigate risks stage* of the buying process is designed to help salespeople build buyer confidence. Salespeople are often having conversations about specific concerns regarding pricing, terms, and implementation. Negotiating with the buyers is a particularly challenging type of sales call at this stage. Entire books are dedicated to the topic of negotiation; however, some of the same rules that apply to the prior stage also apply here. Preparation is key. Coaching matters. It is vital that managers and sellers agree on a negotiation strategy and play out how that strategy is likely to unfold. Development of concession limits and terms must be identified. It is also very useful to role-play these conversations with your salespeople prior to speaking with the buyers.

In addition to negotiation, other types of sales conversations happen at this stage that warrant coaching attention. In this stage, buyer thinking shifts to consideration of the risks they may face in making a change. They want assurance, and they want proof sources. They want to feel safe to move forward. Coaching at this stage can prepare salespeople to empathize with their buyers and acknowledge that other clients had similar concerns. Managers can help their salespeople identify and communicate references, case studies, and other proof sources to mitigate buyer concerns.

EXAMPLE

Coaching Salespeople on Working with Buyers to Mitigate Perceived Risks

Again, I hearken back to my days as a salesperson for Xerox for the perfect example of call coaching for risk mitigation. I was in a sales process with a large law firm. The legal administrator was evaluating my product and one competing alternative. The only problem was that the competitor was offering the *same machine* I was selling but at *half the price*. Xerox had just entered an original equipment manufacturer (OEM) arrangement with another office equipment supplier, and they were selling the exact same machine under their brand. Yikes, this was very bad news.

I approached my sales manager and shared my sad state of affairs. I had been working on this deal for over a year, and it was important to me. It was the difference between just hitting quota and getting to president's club. I wasn't willing to give up. I just didn't know how best to navigate this situation. My sales manager asked me why the client should pay double for the same equipment. He asked me what the law firm would get if they bought from me versus the other company. I told him that they would get me. He wanted to know why that mattered: "So what?"

It mattered because in reality, installation of these large machines almost never went smoothly. Problems surfaced and had to be ironed out. I was very experienced at anticipating issues, dealing with them, and getting them resolved quickly. Hmmm. After about an hour of conversation with my sales manager, I had a plan.

In my next meeting with the legal administrator, she brought up the competitive proposal. She said, "Come on, Michelle, I like you and all, but why on earth should I pay double to buy from you?"

That's when my call coaching came into play. I asked her if she had ever had an installation of one of these machines go smoothly. Ever.

She said no.

I asked if she honestly believed that this time it would be different, that no issues would arise.

She said no, there would probably be issues.

That's when I asked the question my manager and I had prepared. I asked, "Doris, if things go wrong and the installation gets messy, whom do you want by your side—me or the other guy?"

It was a pretty gutsy question, but it was the right one. It worked. Call coaching in action, thanks to my very talented sales manager.

WHERE TO APPLY YOUR CALL COACHING EFFORTS

In Chapter 8 on opportunity coaching, we shared our research findings that high-performing sales managers were much more likely than low performers to focus their coaching efforts on the early stages of the sales cycle.

Does this also hold true for call coaching? What's better, early-stage call coaching or late-stage call coaching? Well, we found that all managers in our study were more likely to *plan* calls in the early stages of the sales cycle. Although this trend was a bit higher for high-performing managers, it was not statistically significant.

As we stated in Chapter 8, we found a significant correlation between early-stage opportunity coaching and performance. We didn't tell you the whole story. We also found that high-performing managers were twice as likely as their lower-performing peers to spend time in their scheduled opportunity coaching discussions *planning upcoming calls*. Figure 9.4 shows the difference in the percentage of high-performing versus low-performing managers who spend dedicated, scheduled time on planning calls. Because these high-performing managers orient their opportunity coaching to early stage, and they spend a portion of that time planning calls, it stands to reason that the call planning they do in those coaching sessions is also targeted at early stage.

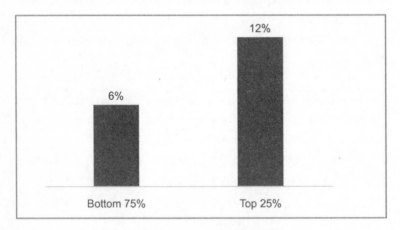

FIGURE 9.4 **Focus on Call Coaching**

Once we understand the interplay between opportunity and call coaching, this makes intuitive sense. Opportunity and call coaching often go hand in hand. The conversations typically unfold in the following ways as indicated in Figure 9.5. We strategize the opportunity and then plan

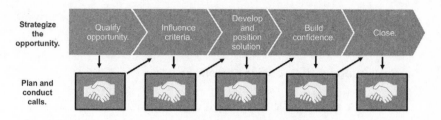

FIGURE 9.5 **Opportunity and Call Management Working Together**

the call. We do this many times across the sales process. The more complex the opportunity, the more rigorous the opportunity *and* call coaching.

STRUCTURING CALL COACHING CONVERSATIONS

Call coaching benefits from deliberate structuring. Some typical inputs, agenda items, and outputs are reflected in Figure 9.6. As we indicated, call coaching is the most tactical of all types of sales coaching. The agenda items reflect this tactical orientation.

Inputs	Agendas	Outputs
• Notes from CRM • Prior account activity • Goals for next sales call	• Agree on call objectives. • Evaluate seller's plan versus customer buying stage. • Anticipate or role play interaction elements. • Clarify agenda, roles, resources, and additional preparation steps.	• Call objectives • Formalized agenda • Documented call plan • Success criteria

FIGURE 9.6 **Common Elements of Effective Call Coaching Discussions**

In addition to agendas, good call coaching questions can drive high levels of collaboration during call coaching conversations. As usual, the most effective call coaching conversations involve a balance of give-and-take between the sales manager and the salesperson. Below is a typical list of early-stage call coaching questions:

Early-Stage Call Coaching Questions

- Where are the buyers in the buying process?

- What is their primary objective at this stage?

- What is the call objective?

- What are the prospects' needs? Buying criteria?

- How do our offerings address their needs?

- What additional information or data is needed?

- What questions will you ask?

- What are potential reactions or objections?

- What materials or resources will you need?

- What is your agenda for the call?

- How will you open the call?

- What will we ask for as next steps?

COACHING FOR BETTER CALL PLANNING

Helping your salespeople *plan* upcoming sales calls is the most important type of call coaching you can do as a sales manager. Regardless of whether you choose to observe any given sales call, that same sales call will most certainly be more effective if the salesperson has a solid plan. If, like most sales managers, time is a precious and scarce resource, allocating your call coaching efforts toward call planning would be a wise choice. Helping your salespeople plan their sales calls sets them up for success. The following process will give you a logical, easy-to-follow process for planning calls with your salespeople:

- **Begin with the end.** The first step in helping your salespeople plan an upcoming sales call is to determine their desired outcome for that interaction. At the end of the interaction, what commitment do they want the buyer to make? Is it for another meeting? Is it for the buyer to arrange a follow-up meeting with another person within the account? Is it for the buyer to gather needed information and provide it to the salesperson? It is important to help the salesperson decide how success of the sales call will be measured and determine what the salesperson will communicate as that next step to the buyer at the end of the conversation. It should feel natural and not forced. The rest of the planning process should support achievement of the desired outcome.

- **Anticipate buyer interests.** The next item for consideration in the planning process is to consider what information is likely to be important to this buyer. Will the buyer want information on the salesperson's solutions? If so, which ones are likely to be relevant? Will the buyer want evidence that the salesperson has done this type of project before? Will the salesperson need case studies or proof sources? A discussion of topics the buyer is likely to be interested in helps the salesperson ensure that he or she has the right type of information to share with the buyer at the right time.

- **Plan to gather information.** Another element of call planning is to determine what type of information the salesperson will want to obtain during the meeting. Some portion of the seller's questions should be targeted at predetermined areas of interest, such as buyer problems and needs. Good questions are necessary to drive collaborative dialogue and help the salesperson avoid jumping too quickly to a discussion of solutions. The best questions are ones that are preplanned and comprehensive.

- **Anticipate objections.** It is useful to help the salesperson consider any possible objections that may arise during the sales call. By exploring potential objections, you can help the salesperson develop strategies to handle these objections. It may be useful to role-play various ways to handle tough objections. This helps build seller confidence and reduces the risk of getting sidetracked during the sales call.

- **Plan the opening.** The last thing to plan is how the salesperson will open the sales conversation. It may seem counterintuitive to plan the opening last; however, it is much easier to figure out how to open the conversation after you've thought through the details of how the conversation will unfold. An effective opening includes some sort of rapport building, a suggested agenda, and an agreement on time allotment for the meeting. The opening should also prime the buyer that a next step will be established at the end of the conversation.

Documenting call planning efforts can be very useful to ensure that salespeople execute calls in a way that reflects the agreed-on approach. Sales managers can use formal call planning worksheets to help guide their call coaching discussions. If you have a call management methodology in place, chances are very high that you have access to an associated call planning worksheet. Call planning worksheets help promote comprehensive coaching, and they improve sales call execution. We provide a sample call planning worksheet in Figure 9.7.

Call planning is a powerful activity and one that leads to better call outcomes. As with most types of sales activities, moderation is warranted. A common mistake managers make is to set expectations for salespeople to plan all sales calls, without taking into consideration the nature of the individual calls. Not all calls are complex enough to warrant comprehensive planning. When managers expect salespeople to develop and document comprehensive plans for all sales calls, performance suffers. Figure 9.8 illustrates that high-performing managers are significantly more likely to require plans for only a subset of sales calls as compared to their lowest-performing peers.

Because this trend toward moderation is significantly related to quota attainment, it warrants further exploration. In many cases organizational-

Sales Call Plan

Call objective or action:

Opening:

Agenda:

Background: We need:
-
-
-

Positioning Capabilities

Key features of our solution:

Benefits to the customer:

Problems our solution solves:	PAIN	Consequences of these problems:	Customer desires our solution address:	GAIN	Additional payoff if desires are met:
-	-		-		-
-	-		-		-

Questions to Ask	Notes

FIGURE 9.7 Sample Call Planning Worksheet

Source: Vantage Point Performance.

level planning requirements impede manager and salesperson effectiveness. One particularly interesting story occurred with Terry, the sales operations director of a global healthcare company. Terry's sales force had recently received extensive sales training aligned to a popular sales methodology. This methodology was designed to teach salespeople how to effectively plan and execute individual sales conversations. This was a *best-in-class* training program that came highly recommended, and it was launched

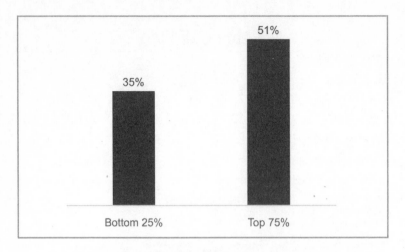

FIGURE 9.8 **High-Performing Managers Require Call Plans for Only a Subset of Calls**

with much fanfare. After the salespeople were trained, a planning metric was instituted. Each salesperson was required to develop and document 10 call plans per week and submit them to their respective sales manager.

Initial compliance fell far fall short of the mark. The salespeople continually complained that call planning was too time-consuming—which is why they were not doing it. To simplify the planning task, the company researched and acquired a very expensive software program designed to automate call planning. This automated call planning was accomplished with an online template that included a series of drop-down menus. Salespeople could complete a call plan in about five minutes. To Terry's delight, compliance improved immediately and dramatically. Great news, right? Well, not so fast.

The automation software sure made the sellers more productive! Individual managers had roughly 10 salespeople reporting to them. That meant they were receiving about 100 documented plans each week. Initially, the managers tried their best to review each plan and provide feedback. After about two weeks, timely feedback on incoming call plans ground to a halt. As you can imagine, the sales managers had precious little time for reviewing call plans, especially *100 of them per week*. None of the leadership team was aware of the issue with this new software, but I suspected the picture was not quite as rosy as believed. The salespeople quickly realized that the call plans were not being evaluated and wisely began to recycle them.

We asked Terry a very simple question, "What was your goal in automating this planning process?"

He looked at us as if we were a bit dull and said, "Well, to get people doing more planning, of course."

We then asked him, "Is the goal more planning or better planning?"

He wasn't initially convinced that there was a difference. As subtly as possible, we suggested that *quantity* of activity doesn't always equal *quality*. We asked if it was possible that the compliance he was experiencing was not actually leading to higher-quality plans. Terry wasn't happy with my suggestion, but it caused him to question the efficacy of the automatic call planning software.

Because we had interviewed a few of the frontline sales managers, we knew that the sheer quantity of plans being submitted meant that very little real inspection of plans and associated coaching and feedback was happening. We pressed the point. We suggested that if Terry could dig into the system archives and identify just a few quality call plans, we could then use them as a benchmark for comparison with other plans. Even a few good call plans could be used to provide empirical support that the system was working. We scheduled a call for the following week to review his findings.

The defining hour had arrived. We were on the phone for the sole purpose of examining Terry's findings. We asked, "Were you able to find a suitable number of effective plans?"

"Well," he replied, "Not exactly."

"Were you able to find at least five good plans, the minimum goal?"

"No, I was not able to find five. I was not able to find one."

We were silent for a minute, digesting the information we just heard. We were unsure how to proceed. We weren't surprised—just unprepared for the degree of failure this poor man had just experienced.

We knew why it wasn't working. When we first saw the tool, we suspected it wouldn't work, but Terry wasn't ready to hear that from us at the time. Unfortunately, we had to lead him down the well-worn path of self-discovery where the desired outcome is not achieved because the path to execution was flawed. He realized that his well-intentioned effort, and the associated failure of quality call planning, proved the point that more is not better, especially if not done well.

This overinflated call planning expectation created a lot of work, for both the salespeople and the sales managers, and it still didn't yield the desired results. This was a "Ready, fire, aim" situation, and it failed. Hundreds of thousands of dollars, and lots of lost credibility later, nothing meaningful had changed. Be mindful of setting realistic expectations with your salespeople. Be clear about the set of conditions that must exist to warrant in-depth call planning.

This example forces the question, "What is the real value in call planning?" Is it to get salespeople thinking? Is it to improve the quality of customer interactions? Is it to bring rich experience to bear to help your salespeople? The answer is yes to all of these questions. The more important point is that helping salespeople plan upcoming sales calls is not just a check-the-box activity. It is one of the highest-impact types of coaching you can provide. If the success of your opportunity pursuit rests on the quality of individual interactions—which it does—than call planning is key.

COACHING THROUGH OBSERVATION AND FEEDBACK

Although call planning is an extremely powerful type of call coaching, call observation has been the primary and preferred method of call coaching. Sales managers often feel that there is no more illuminating way to evaluate the effectiveness of salespeople than to watch them in action with potential buyers. Managers can learn volumes about their salespeople's effectiveness by seeing how they navigate individual sales calls. We can see and hear what salespeople are doing and then give them immediate feedback on what we saw. Since this is a common method of coaching our salespeople, it pays to get it right.

When observing a sales call for coaching purposes, it is useful to have some sort of structure to the observation and associated feedback. Many organizations use formal observation and feedback worksheets that align with their call management process. Having a predetermined structure in mind helps managers capture seller behavior in a way that ensures specific and helpful feedback. Figure 9.9 is an example of a coaching form that can be used to capture seller behaviors and provide a mechanism for feedback and coaching. This specific observation sheet is aligned to a call management methodology called Reflective Selling. If you have a formal call management methodology within your organization, it is likely that you have an observation form aligned to that methodology.

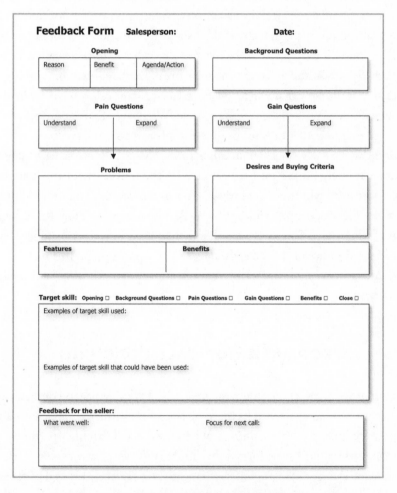

FIGURE 9.9 Sales Call Observation and Feedback Worksheet

Source: Vantage Point Performance.

Structured feedback forms help make it easier for managers to focus their observations to specific types of seller behaviors. Focused observations encourage managers to limit the type and amount of feedback they provide. Without a structure in mind, managers are likely to take very detailed notes (which is good) and then provide feedback on everything they wrote down (which is bad). In situations like this, salespeople become overwhelmed and don't know how to act on the feedback they've been given. Good intentions. Bad outcome.

Another important question to consider is which type of sales calls to attend. Should you attend calls for observation purposes or for joint selling purposes? Well, that depends. As a sales manager, it is highly likely that you will participate in late-stage sales calls. Late-stage calls are the high-risk ones, the ones that make or break the likelihood of winning a deal. It is unlikely that when you attend a late-stage call you will be in observer mode. You will be in *selling* mode. We all are. That's appropriate.

Attending sales calls for purposes of observation and feedback is best done at the early stages of an opportunity. Sales calls at the early stages are extremely important because they set the trajectory for the how the opportunity will unfold; however, they are lower risk and more appropriate for observation and feedback. As illustrated in Figure 9.10, high performers are 15 percent more likely than their lower-performing peers to attend sales calls in the early stages of an opportunity. This reinforces the idea that early-stage calls are most appropriate for observation and feedback.

FORMALITY OF CALL COACHING

Unlike opportunity coaching, the majority of sales managers conduct call coaching on an as-needed basis, regardless of performance level. Initially, we were surprised by this finding. We fully expected that high-performing managers would have a formal rhythm for *all types of sales coaching*. That was not the case. When you dig beneath the surface, this makes sense. Opportunities, especially complex ones, unfold over time. They can take

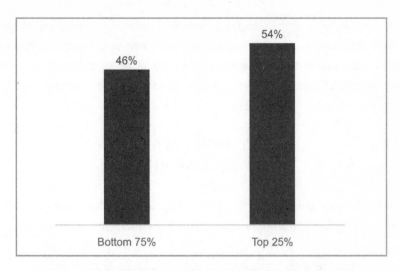

FIGURE 9.10 **High Performers Attend Most Early-Stage Sales Calls**

weeks, months, or sometimes years to close. Sales calls are rarely scheduled months in advance. They are typically scheduled weeks or days in advance. You can't realistically plan a sales call until it is scheduled.

As we mentioned, high-performing sales managers are more likely than low performers to dedicate formally scheduled opportunity coaching time to plan upcoming sales calls; however, in the strictest sense, most call coaching is as needed because of the nature of sales calls. As we indicated earlier in this chapter, high-performing managers are also much more likely to proactively request call planning discussions. This is in line with our findings that high-performing managers are more deliberate and proactive than low-performing managers.

Although most call coaching discussions are not formally scheduled in a repeated pattern, the depth to which these coaching conversations unfold differs between high- and low-performing managers. The most frequently selected time allocation for high-performing managers is between 30 and 60 minutes. Lower-performing managers typically spend under 30 minutes. Although we did not find that more hours of coaching led to higher performance, we did find that spending more time in *each discussion* was correlated to higher performance. Having fewer, but more robust coaching discussions is overall more effective. These seemingly small differences in practices such as proactively requesting call coaching discussions and spending more time in each conversation, when taken together, lead to more effective coaching and more salespeople at quota.

KEY TAKEAWAYS:
CALL COACHING

- The goal of call coaching is to equip salespeople to maximize the effectiveness of individual customer interactions.

- The most successful sales managers proactively request call coaching discussions to plan important sales calls. Less successful sales managers are most likely to plan sales calls that they are attending.

- High-performing sales managers are more likely to request formal call plans for only a subset of sales calls, whereas their lower-performing peers are more likely to request formal plans for all sales calls.

- The most successful sales managers adjust their call coaching efforts to align with the buyers' position in their buying process. As sales activities change, so does relevant call coaching.

- Although all sales managers conduct call coaching on an as-needed basis, high-performing sales managers are more likely to dedicate a portion of their formally scheduled opportunity coaching sessions to this important task.

- Early-stage coaching is directly correlated to higher performance, and top-performing managers are more likely to attend early-stage calls compared with lower performers.

- Low-performing managers spend more time in the field than their high-performing counterparts. Low performers report spending more time in the field than their organization requires. High performers spend about the required amount of time in the field or slightly less.

- Call observation and feedback have been the traditional methods of choice for call coaching; however, feedback tends to be over-done. Using a formal observation tool can ensure that feedback is targeted and actionable.

CHAPTER 10

REALITY IS MESSY: ADAPTING COACHING TO A FEW SPECIAL SITUATIONS

Well, we're almost to the finish line, and we've covered a lot of ground. In the first chapter of this book, we made the case for better sales management and coaching. Sales managers are failing. The percentage of salespeople at quota continues its steady decline. According to Jonathan Farrington, CEO of Top Sales World and editor of *Top Sales Magazine*, 2017 was the first year that the percentage of salespeople at quota dipped below the 50 percent mark. He lamented that this decline has been significant and that roughly 16 percent fewer salespeople are at quota today compared with four years ago. Clearly, we must reverse this trend. Our best chance for getting more salespeople to quota is by improving the effectiveness of our frontline sales managers, and training is a key enabler to that goal.

We've introduced a research-based framework for highly effective sales coaching that, if adopted, will lead to more salespeople at quota. We've even drilled into the specific types of activity coaching you can do as a sales manager and provided detailed guidance on how to determine and execute the best structure and rhythm of coaching. We've given you a blueprint for sales coaching. One that works.

However, as in many areas of life, coaching is not always a cut-and-dried affair. There are often peculiarities and messy realities that must be attended to for effective sales coaching to occur. In this last chapter, we explore a few of these additional considerations to help ensure that the plan you put together for your coaching efforts has the best chance of succeeding. We acknowledge that we cannot cover every possible contingency for effective sales coaching. However, we'll cover a few of the more thorny issues that get in the way of well-intentioned sales managers and impede coaching efforts.

DIFFERENT SALES ROLES, DIFFERENT SALES ACTIVITIES

If you recall from Chapter 4, the first key component of our coaching guidance concerned the creation of a path to get your salespeople to the results you want. By connecting business results to sales objectives, identifying high-impact activities, and creating standards for activity execution, you dramatically improve the quality and consistency of sales execution, as well as create clarity of the sales task.

This guidance is a critical first step to ensure that you set your salespeople and yourself up for success. As you might expect, this is not always a one-size-fits-all proposition. Sometimes sales managers manage more than one role. Other times, they manage a team of people who are in the same sales role but have some unique characteristics that require adjustment. We will deal with each of these situations to clarify the best approach to coaching.

To make this easier to grasp, we will return to an example we've used several times throughout this book. The goal is not for you to understand the exact nature of the roles we describe but, instead, to understand that the roles are *different* and require a *different approach* to sales coaching. We return to the financial services company and the client manager role to begin our discussion. Recall that the client manager role was responsible for growth in the company's *current client base*. The path to results for the client manager is below:

- **Business result:** Year-over-year revenue growth of 5 percent.

- **Sales objective:** Increase new business within existing accounts by 10 percent through expansion of product mix.

- **Sales activities:** Proactive *analysis* of growth opportunities based on analysis of client data. Formal *meeting* with key contacts in each account to review analysis and qualify opportunity for expansion.

Well, much like most global companies, this financial services client had a variety of *different sales roles*. In this next section, we will examine the role of *new business representative* and how the path to clarity of task differed for this second role. The beauty of the results-objectives-activities framework is that it works equally well in all situations. It provides sales managers with a completely flexible prioritization approach that is agnostic to organization or sales role variation.

Let's examine a path to clarity of task for the new business representative in this same client organization. We'll use the following example:

- **Business result:** Year-over-year revenue growth of 5 percent.

- **Sales objective:** Acquire 12 new clients per year per new business salesperson.

- **Sales activities:** Identify 10 target accounts in each of the four industry segments. Develop a prospecting plan for connecting with key contacts in each organization. Develop and deploy targeted messaging for each contact by industry segment.

As you can see, the business result was the same for both the client manager and the new business representative: 5 percent revenue growth year-over-year. The variation tends to begin at the sales objective level. In the case of the new business representative, the sales objective was new account acquisition as opposed to expansion of existing accounts. The sales activities were also markedly different. For the new business representative, activity standards were equally important. We will use the following activity to examine the standards this client set:

Sales activity: Develop and deploy targeted messaging for each contact by industry segment.

Recall that the first element of activity standards involves *how well* an activity is executed, which is the qualitative aspect of standard setting. This client had developed very specific value propositions for their four target industries for new account acquisition. New business representatives had to demonstrate their ability to adapt the industry-specific value propositions to a target client and contact. The value propositions had to be demonstrated in a role-play dialogue with their sales manager, as well as in a tailored e-mail format. Regarding the quantitative standard, or *how much* of the activity must be executed, it was required that each new business representative make contact with at least three prospective accounts per week.

In contrast to the standards set for the client managers, qualitative and quantitative standards had to be established for the new business representatives as well. The results were the same for the new business representatives and the client managers; however, the objectives (Os) and activities (As) were different. Different roles, different paths to results. Clarity of task in action again, but adjusted by role.

CREATING A PATH TO RESULTS: BY ROLE AND BY SALESPERSON

As you can probably deduce by now, identifying which activities salespeople should engage in to improve their chances of hitting quota is not always as straightforward as it might appear. A clear link between activities, objectives, and results is vital to ensure that seller effort is truly productive. Another typical question we get from sales managers related to creating clarity of task is whether they should identify this path to results for each salesperson, or whether they should do it by role. This is an excellent question and one that must be addressed.

We've provided examples of a path to results for two separate sales positions within a financial services firm. The client manager role targeted growth of existing accounts, and the new business representative targeted new account acquisition. It is highly likely that variation also exists within teams of like roles. As a sales manager, it is up to you to determine when and how to deal with this variation. There are also situations in which the characteristics of the sales assignment differ. In such cases, additional adjustments must be made in your coaching approach.

UNIQUE CHARACTERISTICS OF THE SALES ASSIGNMENT

Whether a salesperson is covering a few large accounts, many smaller accounts in a geographic territory, or anything in between, unique characteristics may be present that require adjustment to your management and coaching approach. The economic environment may be different from assignment to assignment, the competitive landscape may be different, or penetration levels may vary widely. Ultimately, there may be significant *variation* between assignments for people in *similar roles*. This often requires that you modify the direction and coaching you provide to your salespeople in these situations.

We will use an example of two sales consultants in a global healthcare company to make this point. Both sales consultants have geographic assignments and are responsible for covering approximately 150 assigned accounts that are a mix of existing customers and prospects. Although both salespeople have a similar job description, the geographies in which they reside involve very different competitors.

Because it is useful to begin the results-objectives-activities (ROA) mapping process at the role level, a common path to results for the sales consultant may look something like the following:

- **Business result:** Quota achievement.

- **Sales objectives:** Increase average selling price (ASP) by 10 percent. Increase sales of premium product A by 10 percent.

- **Sales activities:** Recommend premium product A in all opportunities where product B is currently being sold. Provide training to client staff to recommend antireflective coatings with every prescription filled.

In this case, one sales consultant was in a rural area with few competitors. Price sensitivity was not as relevant. Increasing the average selling price by changing the recommendation from product B to premium product A was a viable approach. However, one of the other sales consultants on the team was in an urban area with intense competition. In this latter case, increasing the average selling price to reach quota was not viable. In this case, the manager had to adjust the sales objectives and associated sales activities to allow for this variation.

For the sales consultant in the urban area with intense competition, getting the customer to change from a less expensive product to a more expensive product was not viable. Because customers in this urban area were much more price sensitive, a more appropriate strategy was to take additional share of wallet from one of the competitors through product replacement. In this case the adjustment in **sales objectives** (*O*s) might be to increase share of wallet by taking 10 percent of a certain product set from a key competitor. An associated high-impact **activity** (*A*) could be to develop and launch a special promotion for customers switching from competitor X's product to a commensurate product offered by the sales consultant. As a sales manager, you must be familiar with the unique characteristics of your salespeople's individual assignments and make appropriate adjustments.

HOW TO ENSURE THAT COACHING HAPPENS

Let's assume that you've identified high-impact activities and standards for the salespeople you manage. You've structured coaching conversations to ensure that the coaching you provide is appropriate and at the right level of depth. Finally, you've determined a workable rhythm for the frequency and duration of your coaching conversations. This is all well and good and will most likely set you up for success. However, there are a few very tricky details that may get in the way if you're not aware of them.

A final, but important consideration is how you will *arrange* your scheduled coaching sessions throughout your week and month. There are some typical traps managers fall into that warrant examination. For example, do you schedule all of your coaching discussions on the same day? Do you schedule them back-to-back with no break in between? Do you schedule your coaching sessions during the times when you are most or least energetic? Do you schedule them on Mondays or Fridays, morning or afternoon? Do you schedule them all in the same week?

There are no absolute right answers to these questions; however, we have found that high-performing managers, those who are able to set a rhythm and execute it consistently, exhibit the following tendencies:

- Schedule coaching sessions on *different days of the week*, say, Monday and Fridays—days least likely to conflict with urgent business demands.

- Schedule different salespeople for *different weeks*—meet with some salespeople midmonth, meet with other salespeople at the beginning or end of the month—allowing more flexibility to meet business demands.

- Schedule *breaks* in between coaching discussions—allowing them to address urgent tasks and reduce stress.

If you look at the above suggestions, you will see that the most effective way to develop a workable rhythm is to *spread your coaching sessions out* over longer periods of time. This increases the likelihood that you will stick to the schedule you've set. It also helps sales managers show up to coaching discussions in a more energetic state. When sales managers try to fit all of their coaching discussions into the same day, they are completely worn out by the time they get through coaching discussion number 4 or 5. Their energy level wanes, their motivation to collaborate declines, and their overall effectiveness plummets.

As a sales manager, if you find yourself dreading your coaching discussions, it is highly likely that you've overscheduled yourself and set yourself up for failure. You can't conduct six or eight back-to-back coaching discussions and be equally effective in all of them. You also can't conduct back-to-back coaching discussions and expect to keep on top of your other duties. Moderation strikes again. Be realistic, know your strengths and limitations, and schedule accordingly.

PUTTING A BOW ON IT

We've examined the most troubling barriers to effective coaching so that you can avoid them. We've provided a research-based method for creating clarity of task for your salespeople by linking their sales activities to the results you want them to achieve. We've provided guidance on the best ways to structure coaching conversations for maximum impact. We've even shared specific research findings and guidance on how to operationalize sales coaching into a workable rhythm.

In addition, we've thoroughly explored the details needed to conduct rich coaching conversations for the four types of sales coaching you can conduct: territory, account, opportunity, and call coaching. We've provided very detailed information to help you structure your sales coaching and develop the right level of formality into your coaching rhythms.

Finally, we've included a few special cases to consider that can help you avoid sales coaching failure.

Our sincere hope is that the sales coaching guidance we've provided is the most practical and useful you've ever received. We hope that we've equipped you to up your coaching game and make a meaningful difference for the salespeople you manage. We've given you specific information that, if used correctly and consistently, will help you be more successful than you ever dreamed—without requiring you to work harder in the process. We know, and have research-based evidence to support, that if you apply what you've learned in this book, you will be a much more effective sales coach.

Our experience with clients gives us confidence that our approach to sales coaching, as detailed in this book, is the most practical and executable method for sales coaching that exists. We sincerely hope that your journey through this book and your own journey as a sales manager and sales coach will be significantly enriched by this guidance. We don't want sales coaching to be a mystery, and we hope our practical guidance has demystified this important part of your job. We wish you much success implementing these practices, and we know that if you do, you will get more of your salespeople to quota—you can truly *Crush Your Quota*.

INDEX

ABOUT THE AUTHORS

 **Michelle Vazzana** is the CEO and a founding part-
ner at Vantage Point Performance, the leading
global sales management training and development firm.

She is a prolific researcher and sought-after
speaker on the topic of sales management and
leadership, having conducted the most extensive
research to date on sales coaching practices. She
has more than 32 years of successful sales and
management experience. Michelle coauthored the bestselling book *Cracking
the Sales Management Code* with Jason Jordan.

Michelle earned a bachelor of science degree in computer science
from Florida International University, a master of science in organizational effectiveness from Marymount Loyola University, and master's
certificates in both instructional systems design and total quality management. Michelle earned her PhD in organizational psychology from
Walden University, with a focus on sales management practices.

Michelle is an avid golfer, and she loves fishing and paddle boarding.
She resides in South Florida with her husband and daughter. For more information, visit www.vantagepointperformance.com.

 **Jason Jordan** is a founding partner of Vantage Point Performance. He is a recognized thought leader in the domain of business-to-business selling, and he conducts ongoing research into management best practices in developing, measuring, and managing world-class sales organizations. Jason's research into sales performance metrics led to the breakthrough insights published in Jason and Michelle's bestselling book *Cracking the Sales Management Code* (McGraw-Hill, 2012).

A popular speaker and writer, Jason is a frequent contributor to the Sales Management Association, the American Society for Training and Development, *Selling Power*, *Sales & Marketing Management*, Salesforce .com, *Forbes*, and other industry groups and publications. He is currently a board member of the Sales Education Foundation, and he is a visiting faculty member in the Executive Education and MBA programs at the University of Virginia's Darden School of Business.

Jason earned an economics degree from Duke University and a master's degree in business administration from the University of Virginia. He resides with his family in Charlottesville, Virginia.

VANTAGEP◆INT

The goal is simple. Sales leaders want a sales team that can **sell the right product, at the right time, to the right customer, using the right approach based on the different situations that it faces.**

Unfortunately, sales leaders have a number of difficult challenges to manage on the road to building a truly effective sales team...**and the risks are high**. Get any one of these wrong and it can mean millions of dollars in both hard dollar costs and lost opportunities.

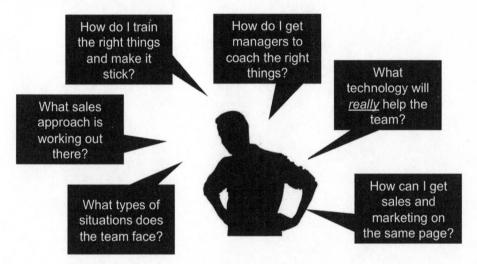

How do I train the right things and make it stick?

How do I get managers to coach the right things?

What technology will *really* help the team?

What sales approach is working out there?

What types of situations does the team face?

How can I get sales and marketing on the same page?

We get it...the Vantage Point team has been there and the good news is that **_we can help with some or ALL of these challenges!_**

> **Vantage Point** offers a variety of services that lead to highly effective sales teams including:
>
> - World class sales force diagnostics and analytics
> - Sales strategy and tactic development
> - Strategy activation through tailored training and reinforcement solutions for both reps and managers
> - CRM and Sales AI advisory services

So, let's just have a conversation to see if we can **make the road to sales effectiveness both easier and shorter** in your sales organization.

 VantagePointPerformance.com

 LinkedIn.com/Company/Vantage-Point-Performance

 @SalesCode